TIANANMEN SQUARE

TIANANMEN SQUARE

THE MAKING OF A PROTEST

A DIPLOMAT LOOKS BACK

VIJAY GOKHALE

HarperCollins *Publishers* India

First published in India by
HarperCollins *Publishers* in 2021
A-75, Sector 57, Noida, Uttar Pradesh 201301, India
www.harpercollins.co.in

2 4 6 8 10 9 7 5 3

Copyright © Vijay Gokhale 2021

P-ISBN: 978-93-5422-535-2
E-ISBN: 978-93-5422-536-9

The views and opinions expressed in this book are the author's own and the facts are as reported by him, and the publishers are not in any way liable for the same.

Vijay Gokhale asserts the moral right
to be identified as the author of this work.

All rights reserved. No part of this publication may be reproduced, stored in a retrieval system, or transmitted, in any form or by any means, electronic, mechanical, photocopying, recording or otherwise, without the prior permission of the publishers.

Typeset in 11.5/15.4 Minion Pro at
Manipal Technologies Limited, Manipal

Printed and bound at
Replika Press Pvt. Ltd.

MIX
Paper from
responsible sources
FSC® C016779

This book is produced from independently certified FSC® paper to ensure responsible forest management.

The leaders are aware that what happened is an extremely ugly mark on their historical record, and they have been eager to have the world forget it as soon as possible.

Fang Lizhi

Contents

Preface ix

Prologue xi

1 The Principal Player 1
2 The Remaining Cast 14
3 Storm Clouds on the Horizon 20
4 Strong Winds 30
5 The Lull 41
6 The Spark 56
7 Conflagration 69
8 The Blaze 88
9 Dousing the Flames 103
10 Doubling Down 131

Epilogue 143

Notes 151

Acknowledgements 165

Selected Bibliography 167

Index 169

About the Author 183

Preface

I HAVE ALWAYS WANTED TO TELL THIS STORY SINCE I WITNESSED IT thirty-one years ago in Beijing, but my circumstances prevented me from doing so until now.

It has been called by many names, but is best known as the Tiananmen Square incident because Tiananmen Square was the stage on which the drama that held the world spellbound for fifty days was performed. The happenings in the square led to the sort of chaos and uncertainty that usually presages a regime change. That did not happen.

At the time it was a global phenomenon. Within a few months, however, the Berlin Wall came down and the world's attention reverted to Europe. The happenings in China in the spring and early summer of 1989 faded from public memory.

A few writers, most Western, wrote accounts from their perspective. Soon business trumped politics and even these accounts dried up. Inside China a massive cover-up that started immediately after the end of the crisis, has blanked out any memories except those that the Chinese Communist Party wants its people to know.

There was a brief revival of interest in the early years of the 2000s, when tapes recorded by the former general secretary Zhao Ziyang found their way to Hong Kong. It was his version of the truth, and was intended to prove his innocence.

In the fifty days that the drama played out in Tiananmen Square, there was no serious effort by the Indian media to cover the happenings. Two intrepid young media persons from *India Today* – Shekhar Gupta and Prashant Panjiar – were the only people to cover the events in Beijing. The larger story has remained untold from the Indian perspective.

This is a story that needs telling because China is our neighbour and our people require a much deeper understanding of China than is presently the case. My story is intended to interpret the facts, to some of which I was eyewitness, with the benefit of hindsight. While thirty years have passed, it still remains an event of seminal importance in recent Chinese history. China has changed, yet the communist system remains. Personalities have come and gone, but the Red Aristocracy still rules China and stays focussed on self-preservation and self-perpetuation. Indians can no longer afford to have a superficial understanding of events involving their largest neighbour and to-be-hegemon, other than at their own peril.

Prologue

In early April Beijing can still be very cold but nowadays the skies are not the kind of cerulean as they used to be in 1989. Those days there were thousands of bicycles on the roads but few cars, so that it was possible to walk on the Avenue of Eternal Peace from the Jianguo Gate to the Tiananmen Square without any serious threat to life or limb. Greys and blues were still the dominant colours among the Chinese. Fraternization between Chinese and foreigners, though not forbidden, was uncommon and discouraged. We lived in compounds guarded by the People's Armed Police, not so much to protect us as, it seemed, to prevent the ordinary Chinese from entering these compounds. The *waiguoren* (foreigners) were privileged persons, with special shops for groceries and the Friendship Store stocked with Chinese handicrafts, and they even had special money, the Foreign Exchange Certificate, known in Chinese as *waihui*, to buy things not available to the ordinary Chinese.

PROLOGUE

Beijing Capital Airport had two small circular terminals and an antiquated arrival hall. Most people still travelled on trains. From the airport there was a single-lane road into the city, lined with old trees and largely rural. The road met the city at the Third Ring Road (there are now seven), where the traveller was met with rows upon rows of Soviet-style apartments. Most buildings were old and unpainted, and few were taller than five stories since there were no elevators. The tiny balconies were stuffed high with *bai cai*, the ubiquitous white cabbage that was a winter staple and could be stored in the outdoors for several weeks. Behind the Great Hall of the People, where the National Opera House now stands, were the courtyard houses (*siheyuan*) for which Beijing was famous. These were, at one time, when Beijing was an imperial capital before 1911, the residences of the nobility and mandarins in the service of the Chinese emperors, but were now occupied by many families. The main roads were broad, especially the Avenue of Eternal Peace, which Mao had widened by destroying ancient city walls and buildings that had stood for centuries, for his grand parades and mass campaigns. Two ring roads encircled the city, the first of the two encompassing the Old City of Beijing, and traditional gates such as the Jianguomen and the Deshengmen were still preserved. Beyond these main roads, most of Beijing still had narrow lanes that were densely populated, some too narrow for even a car to traverse, and hidden amongst them were faded gems of Chinese architecture in red and ochre with yellow imperial dragon tiles. Despite the run-down appearance, the city was spotlessly clean, public transport was available and the children looked in rude good health.

The leadership lived and worked in the western wing of the Forbidden City, the imperial palace of the Ming and Qing emperors, in pavilions and houses that ranged around two man-made lakes – the Central and the South – from which it got its name, the Zhongnanhai. The formal entrance to the complex was through the Xinhuamen, or the New China Gate, located on the Avenue of Eternal Peace, but the leaders themselves drove in black limousines with tinted windows through smaller gates in the western wall of the Forbidden City. They had summer homes in the Western Hills just outside the city. The Zhongnanhai complex was guarded by the People's Armed Police. It was out of bounds for the ordinary Chinese.

There were few shops, no malls and no real public entertainment. Wangfujing and Xidan were shopping streets, tree-lined and with state-run stores. Power cuts were not infrequent. Staple foods were never in short supply, but luxuries could not be had by the Chinese. There were few foreign-run hotels including the Jianguo and the Jinglun, both on the Avenue of Eternal Peace which was the main east–west axis of the capital city. In the summer, temperatures reached up to 40 degrees Celsius, and most Beijingers spent the evenings out of doors, the men usually with their upper garment hitched above the chest to ward off the heat. Many found respite in the public parks bearing lovely names like Altar of the Moon, Purple Bamboo and Taoran Pavilion, and these were the pride and joy of the city. These parks were the go-to place to exercise, play and indulge in Western ballroom dancing. These were also virtually the only places that foreigners could meet and converse with the Chinese. The parks had beautiful lakes which allowed for boating in the summers and ice skating in the winters. Spring in these parks was particularly beautiful – with forsythia, magnolia, plum, peach and cherry blossoms, especially in the Beihai (Northern Sea), which was an imperial park.

There were three diplomatic compounds in Beijing in those days, and all diplomats and foreign media were compelled to live there if they did not have residential quarters in their chanceries. We had an apartment in the Qijiayuan diplomatic compound with a balcony that opened directly on to the Avenue of Eternal Peace, some four kilometres from Tiananmen. It was to prove fortuitous in the early summer of 1989 when the Avenue of Eternal Peace became a vast open-air ramp along which all the actors in the drama that came to be called the Tiananmen Square incident, paraded, cycled or drove, to the final tragic ending. We had, so to speak, a ring-side seat to the grand theatre, but in early 1988 the balcony was nothing more than a convenient outdoor refrigerator to store food stuff that might otherwise spoil in the heated interiors of the apartment.

Ten years after the end of the Great Proletarian Cultural Revolution unleashed by Mao, that had devastated China in every possible manner and at a staggering human cost,[1] the policy known as the Four Modernizations – the modernization of agriculture, industry, science and technology, and national defence – was steering the world's most populous nation on the path of economic recovery and growth. From 1977 China's GDP grew by at least 7 per cent annually, and, more often than not, in double digits. The starting point was the household contract responsibility system that restored farmers' rights to retain produce and profit. It was followed by changes to industrial policy by introducing the Law on Chinese-Foreign Equity Joint Ventures, to allow foreign companies to manufacture in China with flexible wage structures and by allowing companies to retain profits. It spelt the end of experiments with the people's ownership of all means of production. Per capita incomes doubled in ten years from US$160 in 1977 to US$305 by 1987, and while this might appear insubstantial in absolute numbers, in China this was nothing short of a miracle.

The miracle-maker was a diminutive, tobacco-chewing, diehard communist who played bridge. His name was Deng Xiaoping, and since his story in linked with the Tiananmen Square incident, it is necessary to recount it, to better understand what happened in the fateful summer of 1989. But he was by no means the only player in the drama that was to unfold; the fates and fortunes of so many others were also linked to it, that a brief introduction of the players becomes necessary.

:CHAPTER 1:

The Principal Player

DENG XIAOPING WAS BORN UNDER A DIFFERENT NAME IN SICHUAN province in August 1904, when the Son of Heaven, the Guangxu emperor, ninth in the line of Qing emperors, still ruled from the Forbidden City. China was in the midst of what came to be known as the Century of Humiliation, as the Western Powers encroached on Chinese ports and markets in search of profit, leaving what had been in 1820 the world's largest economy impoverished and on the verge of collapse. It came, therefore, as no surprise when in 1911 the Chinese military deposed the last boy-emperor Pu Yi and declared China to be a republic. Almost immediately, the central authority began to disintegrate and as national unity progressively crumbled, local governors and generals became warlords, though they continued to nominally acknowledge the central authority not dissimilar to the situation that had prevailed in Mughal India following the death of Emperor Aurangzeb.

It was a time of famine, civil war and frequent changes of government. The urban elites and rural landlords continued as before, while the rural Chinese lived as virtual serfs. Poverty and social distress were visible everywhere. Like others of his generation, Deng carried these images when he travelled to France in 1920 under a work-study programme. Europe was in the throes of political transformation. The collapse of the four empires in 1918 had triggered a fierce political competition between the conservative right and the increasingly militant left with its base in organized labour. Deng did a series of jobs and witnessed the casual contempt with which the Europeans treated the Chinese. Deng was to later say that, 'The bitterness of life and the humiliating treatment by foremen or capitalist running dogs had exerted a deep impact upon me.'[1] Deng's biographer, Ezra Vogel, writes that from this point on Deng's persona was inseparable from the national effort to rid China of the humiliation it had suffered. He segued from the Socialist Youth League to the European branch of the newly established Communist Party of China, commonly known as the Chinese Communist Party, in 1924, where his exceptional organizational abilities soon came to the fore.[2] His French sojourn was also important for another reason – he met Zhou Enlai. Together they were destined to steer China in a historic transformation by the end of the twentieth century.

Deng had a brief stopover in Soviet Russia before he involved himself in the civil war against the Chinese Nationalists led by Generalissimo Chiang Kai-shek. It was only in 1927 that he changed his name to Deng Xiaoping. He joined Mao Zedong on his Long March – actually a tactical retreat – to his base in Yan'an in 1935, and for the next fourteen years, from 1936 to 1949, he became the political commissar of the 129th Division of the Eighth Route Army, fighting first against the Japanese and then against Chiang Kai-shek. His partner was the one-eyed general Liu Bocheng, and together they commanded what came to be called as the Liu–Deng Army. It was during these years that Deng organized mass mobilization and earned the respect of the People's Liberation Army.[3] In later life Deng's military credentials were to save both his life and his legacy.

It was in his military years that Deng was also to get acquainted with two other players who would play important roles in the Tiananmen Square incident in 1989. One was Zhao Ziyang, who first met Deng in 1938 when he was a Party functionary in the Hebei-Shandong-Henan region of central China. The other was Hu Yaobang, who served as a political commissar in Sichuan province as part of the Liu–Deng Army.

When their revolution succeeded it was only natural that Deng, who was close to both Mao Zedong and Zhou Enlai who were now the acknowledged faces of the new communist state, should enter national politics. By 1956 Deng was the secretary general of the Central Committee and a member of the politburo. He was just forty-two years of age and was ranked fourth in the communist pantheon after Mao, Liu Shaoqi and Zhou. There were indications that Mao saw Deng's potential early on. Deng subordinated himself to Mao even if he had misgivings on some of the chairman's economic ideas.[4] When Mao made China take a 'great leap forward' in 1958, Deng never openly questioned it, though his contrarian views were known. In the matter of politics, the Communist Party, of which Mao was the face, came above everything else. His loyalty to the principle that the Party was supreme was on display during Mao's vicious campaign against Marshal Peng Dehuai, a highly respected general and China's defence minister, who had criticized Mao's policy of the Great Leap Forward. After Mao attacked Peng at the Lushan Conference in August 1959 and removed him from party and government positions, Deng remained conspicuously silent[5] (he was conveniently absent at Lushan). Such silence was to prove costly to Deng later, and deadly to several other top Chinese leaders when it was their turn to face Mao's wrath in 1966 during the Cultural Revolution, but for Deng the Party was everything and doubts he might have harboured about Mao's political judgement were perhaps sublimated to the larger communist cause.

It was during his early years in power that Deng expounded on his core economic ideas and his political beliefs. Those who expressed surprise over Deng's policy of economic reform and opening up after 1978, and on the ruthless suppression of dissent in the larger political interest of the Party after 1989, need look no further than two major speeches that he delivered in 1962.

Speaking at the Enlarged Working Conference convened by the Party's Central Committee[6] on 6 February 1962, Deng defined his understanding of 'inner-party democracy'. He said that while the frank airing of views inside the Party were to be encouraged, 'factional activities are banned', and he called on the Party to pay heed to 'collective leadership and the division of responsibility'. Democracy was acceptable only within the boundaries defined by the Party high command.

A few months later in July of the same year, in his address to the Communist Youth League on 7 July 1962, Deng put forward his core economic ideas.[7] He said, 'We must set about restoring agricultural production if we want to overcome difficulties … If we fail in agriculture there will be no hope of success in industry …' He went on to add, 'It seems to me that the problems of agriculture must be solved mainly through changes in the relations of production. This means arousing the peasants' initiative.' These ideas became the core of what would become known to the rest of the world in 1980 as the household contract responsibility system, and in reviving China's agriculture as the basis of its industrial modernization. It was here that Deng also referred to the proper management of markets and prices and it is to the Communist Youth League that Deng first spoke those famous words: 'It does not matter if it is a yellow cat or a black cat as long as it catches mice.' Deng's efforts to modernize and reform China after 1978, and his ruthless suppression of 'democracy' in 1989 were not of whim and fancy. The beliefs behind such actions lay at the very core of his being, as was evident from his speeches in 1962.

The Cultural Revolution, launched by Mao in mid-1966 and ending almost a decade later, was a dark period in the history of the Chinese Communist Party. Mao spared no one; presidents, marshals of the People's Liberation Army, ministers, party colleagues and their families and even Mao's friends – all perished, some after suffering physical cruelties and prolonged periods of incarceration. Deng was the second most important target after President Liu Shaoqi, and thus labelled the 'second capitalist roader'; he was exiled to the countryside and his family suffered at the hands of the Red Guards, groups of militant urban youths, whose casual cruelty resulted in permanent injury to Deng's elder son.[8] Even by the standards of the Cultural Revolution, Deng's story is one of exceptional personal and political resilience. He was perhaps the only Chinese leader who returned to government in 1973 when China was teetering on the verge of economic catastrophe, only to be purged again in 1976 after being accused of opportunism and of stirring up the 'right deviationist wind'.

In January 1976, the Chinese premier Zhou Enlai died of cancer. The Gang of Four, powerful members of a radical political faction headed by Mao's wife, Jiang Qing, probably saw an opportunity to remove Deng, who by late 1975 had begun to push Chairman Mao to review the most egregious victimizations of the Cultural

Revolution. In late March the *Wenhui Bao*, a publication based in Shanghai which was a stronghold of the Gang of Four, led with an article not only criticizing Deng, but also denigrating Zhou Enlai. Suddenly, it seemed as if the pent-up grief and sufferings of the Chinese people during the ten years of the Cultural Revolution had reached their limits and exploded into public view on 4 April 1976. It was the Qing Ming Festival – the day when the Chinese pay respect to their ancestors by sweeping their graves and which is considered sacred even by the communists. The Chinese people decided to lay wreaths in honour of Zhou Enlai in Tiananmen Square. The so-called Gang of Four had the wreaths removed, sparking mass anger and huge public demonstrations in the Square the following morning. Mao's henchmen moved swiftly to crush the outrage. Then, on 7 April, Deng was summarily removed from all his party and government positions for a second time in ten years.[9] He was accused of being a bourgeois, a capitalist and, most damningly, of leading the 'counterrevolutionary political incident at Tiananmen'.[10] He escaped with his life because his military friends, especially Marshal Ye Jianying, sheltered him in the southern province of Guangdong.

Six months later the situation had changed dramatically. Mao was dead and the Gang of Four had been overthrown. Mao's anointed successor, Hua Guofeng, an obscure communist who had rapidly risen in Cultural Revolution China simply because he was loyal and unquestioning, was now the party chairman. From the moment Mao died, Deng became the leader-in-exile. Deng plotted his return carefully. Mao had cast a long shadow over China even in death. He couldn't very well attack Mao, but he could use Mao's methods to attack him. He first had himself reinstated in all his party and military positions at the Third Plenary Session of the Tenth Central Committee in July 1977 through a formal resolution. Then at the Eleventh National Congress in August 1977, 'new freedoms' were rewritten into the Party and the state constitutions, presumably with his tacit concurrence, including the freedom to put up big-character posters (known to Chinese as *dazibao*). These are handwritten posters done with ink and brush and have traditionally been tools of protest as well as of political communication. Mao had made use of them in the past to great effect, including on 5 August 1966, when his big-character poster – 'Bombard the Headquarters' (*bao da siling bu*) – gave the signal to his supporters to launch an attack on top leaders like Deng and Liu Shaoqi. Deng was not a fan of such methods, but since the Central Committee had, on 8 August 1966, itself approved 'the fullest use of big-character posters and great debates',[11] Mao's anointed successor may have found it difficult to immediately demur with such a proposal as writing it into the constitution. Deng, therefore, decided to use it as a means to publicly criticize Mao's successor, Hua Guofeng, without directly appearing to have a hand in it.

To the west of Tiananmen Square is Xidan. Today it is one of Beijing's most iconic shopping streets. In the autumn of 1978 this is where the big-character posters first began to appear in a place subsequently known as Democracy Wall. The posters called for change, reform and support to Deng Xiaoping, first indirectly and then directly. On 27 November 1978 people marched from Xidan to Tiananmen Square in support of Deng. Given that the last such demonstration in Tiananmen in April 1976 had been labelled as 'counterrevolutionary' by the Party, and also that this label had still not been removed, it was all the more significant when Deng personally told a delegation from Japan's Democratic Socialist Party that this action was 'legal'. Deng was thus subtly aligning himself with 'public opinion' in order to bring pressure on Chairman Hua Guofeng, and thus giving himself greater room for manoeuvrability on the eve of the historic Third Plenary Session of the Party Congress (meeting of the entire Central Committee of the Party) in the second half of December 1978.

At this session, Deng began the work of remaking modern China. The Party declared that the 1976 Tiananmen protest had never been a 'counterrevolutionary political incident' and was in fact 'completely revolutionary'.[12] Since Deng had been identified in 1976 as the principal instigator and fallen into disgrace during the Cultural Revolution, he was fully rehabilitated after Mao's death when the movement was invalidated. The plenum also decided to shift emphasis away from class struggle on to the cause of 'socialist modernization'. This again seemed to be an indirect undermining of Mao and his successor. Mao had wanted mass struggle to continue and his successor had clothed himself in Mao's cloak with the famous 'Two Whatevers' – uphold whatever policy Mao had made and unswervingly carry out whatever Mao instructed. The plenum, to the contrary, swerved away by deciding to focus instead on the Four Modernizations which it declared to be a 'profound and extensive revolution'. This party conference was noteworthy for another reason. Deng had begun to put into action his plan for leadership changes with the induction of Hu Yaobang into the politburo – the person who would spark off the Tiananmen crisis eleven years later.

One complication did, however, arise around the time the plenum met and took important decisions. A big-character poster appeared in Xidan titled 'The Fifth Modernization'. It was written by Wei Jingsheng, and his words were ominous: 'The leaders of our nation must be informed that we want to take our destiny into our own hands. We want no more gods or emperors. No more saviours of any kind. We want to be masters of our own country, not modernized tools for the expansionist ambitions of dictators.'

This time the target was neither Mao nor his chosen successor Hua Guofeng; it was unmistakably Deng. Recognizing that the Democracy Wall had met his political objective and perceiving the threats it might pose in his rise to power, Deng moved to close it down.[13] In early 1979 the Democracy Wall in Xidan was moved to Yuetan Park. Wei Jingsheng was arrested on March 1979, and in October he was sentenced to fourteen years' imprisonment. Soon after Wei's arrest, Deng outlined the Four Cardinal Principles to underpin the absolute supremacy of the Chinese Communist Party, and to signal to other potential 'Weis' that any challenge to the Party's supremacy was strictly out of bounds. In such matters Deng was ruthless. Neither the constitution nor the fact of having used the Democracy Wall to regain power deterred him.[14] On 7 December 1979 the *New York Times* reported that 'a thin grey line of free expression called Democracy Wall was abolished today by the authorities after a year in which it was plastered with wall posters by dissidents and petitioners criticizing China's leaders …' And just months later, in February 1980, the very party that had, in 1977, declared big-character posters to be a fundamental right, just as wilfully proposed to the National People's Congress that 'the stipulation in Article 45 of the constitution that citizens have the right to speak out freely, air their views fully, hold great debates and with big-character posters, be deleted'. Dissent ceased to be a political tool once Deng returned to power.

The plenum on February 1980 completed the leadership changes that Deng had begun in 1978. It appointed Hu Yaobang as the general secretary of the Communist Party. It appointed Zhao Ziyang as member of the Politburo Standing Committee (he would be appointed as premier in September 1980). It enacted the Guiding Principles for Inner-Party Political Life that upheld 'collective responsibility' and opposed 'arbitrary decision-making'. Mao's legacy was dismantled. Hua Guofeng became irrelevant.[15]

Deng was now China's supreme leader. He was ready to perform his miracle.

He began with economic reform. Deng's imprimatur is visible in virtually every aspect of life in the first half of the 1980s, though nowhere was this more evident than on the economy. It seemed to follow a plan, but Deng readily admitted that he was trying to 'cross the river by feeling the stones'. Nonetheless, it was not entirely ad hoc; the ideas he had expounded in 1962 became the guiding principles of reform. He began, as he had always said he would, by reforming agriculture and by giving the farmer the right to decide what would be produced and to keep the profit. It created the surplus available for investment and released a pool of labour for new employment, both of which spurred the growth of township and village industries in the early 1980s.[16] In 1980, Deng decided to open up selected coastal cities in the two provinces that, historically, served as gateways to the outside world – Guangdong and Fujian. The special economic zones (SEZs) in Shenzhen, Shantou, Zhuhai and Xiamen attracted foreign capital, technology and management into export-oriented manufacturing units, just in time to absorb the surplus rural labour, and these SEZs, in turn, created further pressure for reform in other areas, including the banking sector. Xi Zhongxun, father of President Xi Jinping, steered the most successful of these special economic zones in Shenzhen, just across the border from the British Crown Colony of Hong Kong.[17] Credit must go to Deng for breaking with traditional thinking that the re-entry of foreign enterprises into China would lead to its recolonization. He also broke another shibboleth by decentralizing decision-making, thus allowing provinces, municipalities and local governments to play the role of entrepreneurs. By 1983 the growth in rural incomes created new demand for consumer products, and Deng brought in the factory manager responsibility system into state-owned enterprises to make them entrepreneurial and by empowering them to retain a share of the profits for their business expansion. The strategy was brilliant – it pushed for marketization rather than for privatization – and was intended to retain control of the economy while giving free play to entrepreneurial talent.

The cumulative impact of the reforms began to show quick results. Consumption rose sharply. In percentage terms, consumption in clothing by 1988 was 152 per cent over that in 1978, the consumption of pork and poultry had increased by 194 per cent and 438 per cent, respectively, during the same period, and purchase of bicycles had registered a 395 per cent increase. The Party made it known that white goods, including washing machines, were not bourgeois or decadent, and were, in fact, proletarian. In 1981, only one in five households owned a refrigerator and six households per hundred owned a washing machine. By 1990, half the households had refrigerators and nearly three quarters of them had washing machines.[18]

The improvement in people's living conditions was mirrored by China's longest period of real political stability in the twentieth century. The Chinese people had grown weary of continuous political campaigns and mass agitation for thirty years. They yearned for stability and normalcy. Deng created a new style of politics. He began by refusing to take the post of chairman of the Chinese Communist Party, as much a signal to the people that he was breaking with Maoism as reassuring the people that he was in command and didn't need titles to show it. In fact, the Twelfth Party

Congress in September 1982 would abolish the very post of party chairman. His idea of collective leadership not only removed the capriciousness and arbitrariness inherent in individual leadership, but united the Party behind him. Other communist leaders like Chen Yun, Li Xiannian, Wang Zhen, Ye Jianying, Yang Shangkun, Peng Zhen, Bo Yibo, Xi Zhongxun and Wan Li, collectively known as the Elders, backed him. Deng was able to steer fundamental Party reforms in the early 1980s without serious opposition or struggle. He brought in a succession plan for orderly generational change in leadership, abolished lifelong tenures for all cadres and insisted on collective responsibility.[19] He led by personal example, stepping away from government and party positions as the 1980s progressed so that other veterans would have to do likewise. He tactically conceded ground where necessary. On economic issues he deferred to Chen Yun, and on ideological matters it suited him to allow others like Deng Liqun and Hu Qiaomu to take the lead in the fight against 'bourgeois liberalization' and the promotion of 'socialist spiritual civilization'. So long as any policy served Deng's fundamental goal of strengthening the Party, Deng went along with it, and just as calculatedly he stepped in when the opposite was the case. For Deng, the Communist Party was always first, last and everything, and all else was subordinate to this principle.

In this golden period, Deng also deftly re-crafted China's foreign policy and external image. Before Deng China had swung between the Soviet Union and the United States, and he did a superb balancing act by normalizing relations with Washington in 1979 and following it up with a similar action with Moscow exactly one decade later. He compelled the British to talk to him about the return of Hong Kong. With India too, Deng reached out early in June 1980 when he proposed in an interview to the editor of *Vikrant*[20] that India and China should resolve the boundary question that had plagued relations for two decades through a 'package deal', and later by greeting Prime Minister Rajiv Gandhi when he visited China in December 1988 with the words, 'I welcome you to China, my young friend.'

In early 1985, Deng decided to begin withdrawing from matters of day-to-day governance. He felt that China was set on the road to modernization and prosperity. He wanted to ensure that his work would be continued by the new leadership while he was still alive and under his guidance. With the political transition completed, he saw no reason for anxiety or uncertainty. He prepared to hand over greater responsibilities to his heirs – Hu Yaobang and Zhao Ziyang.

:CHAPTER 2:

The Remaining Cast

Hu YAOBANG WAS BORN IN NOVEMBER 1915 IN A PEASANT FAMILY AND joined the Chinese Communist Party as a member of its Youth League in 1933. His association with Deng went back four decades. He had served under Deng as a political commissar in the Second Field Army during the anti-Japanese war and the civil war that followed, and had followed him to Sichuan after the 'liberation' in 1949 where Deng was the head of the south-western bureau. When Deng was called to Beijing in 1952, Hu went along and became the head of the Communist Youth League (CYL). The CYL was, and continues to be, a stepping stone to higher offices in the Party. Even in the early days, Hu showed that he was a risk taker. He protected intellectuals and academics during Mao's persecution of the so-called rightist intellectuals in the 1950s. Like many others, he suffered during the Cultural Revolution and was sent to do hard labour.

When Deng became the supreme leader in 1978, he had plans for Hu Yaobang, but the dizzying heights to which Hu was suddenly propelled in 1980 astounded Deng's compatriots and detractors alike. He was initially tasked with rehabilitating the thousands of cadres who had been persecuted during the Cultural Revolution. He did this work fearlessly. In quick succession, Deng promoted Hu Yaobang to the politburo and its standing committee at the end of 1978, and to the position of general secretary of the Communist Party in February 1980. Hu became Deng's sword arm in the Party, rebuilding it from the ashes of the Cultural Revolution, and institutionalizing its functioning under Deng's guidance. He continued to take political risks. In particular, he encouraged debate on the political and ideological questions that tested the Party's limits of tolerance. By 1983, powerful leaders were becoming progressively uncomfortable with Hu Yaobang's political ideas.[1] They were unhappy with his strong pushback on the ideological front against conservatives in the Party, his crusade against corruption that targeted families of high-ranking leaders, and his off-the-cuff policy pronouncements on Taiwan, Sino-American relations and even the dining etiquette of the Chinese people. It was to put him on a collision course with his peers in the years ahead, but in early 1985 he enjoyed Deng Xiaoping's complete trust and confidence.

At around the time that Hu joined the Party, another future leader, Zhao Ziyang, also joined the Communist Youth League in 1932. His association with Deng before and after the 1949 Revolution was superficial, but his style of economic management came to Deng's notice. With outsized black spectacles covering his face, he gave the appearance of an academic, but what he lacked in terms of personality was more than made up in terms of competence. When he was the party secretary of Guangdong in 1965, he had begun experimenting with agricultural reform and productivity enhancement. His experiments were interrupted during the Cultural Revolution, but Zhao suffered far less than Deng or Hu, and was rehabilitated by 1971. It was when he was appointed as the party secretary in Sichuan, China's most populous province and known as its 'rice bowl', in 1975, that Zhao gave full play to his experience and knowledge of reforms in both agriculture and industry. He authorized enterprises to retain a share of the profit for further investment or worker bonuses, he permitted bank loans to small private businesses and he allowed enterprises to sell in the open market, output that exceeded their quota. Deng brought Zhao Ziyang to Beijing and turned his experiments in Sichuan into a blueprint for China's economic transformation. Like Hu, Zhao rose quickly, entering the Politburo Standing Committee in 1979, and becoming the premier of the State Council of China by September 1980.

With Deng in charge, his two protégés began to deliver Deng's dream of economic reform and opening China up to the outside world. The rural and enterprise reforms put China on the path to high growth rates by the mid-1980s. Although the results were not linear – indeed, China went through cyclical highs and lows – the progress was evident and Deng expected the trajectory to continue. Hu and Zhao were very different people. Hu was outspoken, Zhao circumspect; Hu was bold, Zhao gave the appearance of being non-threatening; Hu took risk and was unafraid to challenge the veteran revolutionaries, Zhao was, outwardly, more respectful of the Elders. Zhao also took advantage of Hu's temperament to subtly undermine him. If Hu inadvertently strayed into areas of his responsibility, such as Sino-American relations, Zhao would gently chide him, aware that this was being watched by Hu's detractors. Zhao also seemingly harboured a secret desire for great power.

If Hu Yaobang was a peasant and Zhao the son of landed gentry, Li Peng was a 'prince'. Born to a revolutionary parent who lost his life fighting for the 'cause' in the early 1930s, he gained from being not merely a martyr's child but also the adopted son of Zhou Enlai. Li Peng lived and studied in the revolutionary base at Yan'an from 1941 to 1945, before going for higher studies in engineering in the Soviet Union from 1948 until 1954, a privilege given to a chosen few. Li became a power-sector bureaucrat.[2] Under the protection of Zhou Enlai he remained shielded from the cruelties of the Cultural Revolution which befell other princelings, including Deng's own children. In the new age that followed the Cultural Revolution, Li continued his ascent up the power and water ministries as vice minister in the early 1980s and later as minister for the State Education Commission in 1985. Beetle-browed with black-framed glasses and a perpetual sneer on his lips, he was an apparatchik. He had shown none of the reformist zeal of Zhao or the political chutzpah of Hu. He endeared himself to the Elders, especially Chen Yun, with whom he came in contact since the latter supervised all economic policy. It probably helped that he enjoyed Zhou Enlai's posthumous blessings. Li Peng's age and technocratic experience also fitted in with Deng's plan to bring in younger and better-educated technocrats to implement his Four Modernizations.

Li Peng was fortunate to be the right man and at the right place and time. He entered the politburo in 1985, and its standing committee in 1987. His entry on to the national stage as vice premier happened to coincide with a cyclical economic downturn. Economic policy and wage-and-price reforms became the battleground. Lines were drawn and sides were taken. He positioned himself well. Yet, in 1985, it would hardly have been possible to predict that Li Peng would play one of the central roles in the Tiananmen Square incident, earning epithets that would stay with him for the remainder of his life.

Though by early 1985 Deng had raised younger people to high positions in the Party and the state, those who had fought and lived through the war of liberation and survived the capriciousness and cruelty of Mao Zedong remained politically active. Known as the Elders, they had stopped the Gang of Four from seizing power after Mao's demise in September 1976 and had also been instrumental in Deng's return. In exchange for a share of power despite their age, and privileges for their families, these veterans had backed Deng's policy of Four Modernizations.[3] They still regarded themselves as vanguards of the revolution and as defenders of the communist 'faith'. And they took this responsibility very seriously.

Many of them had died during the Cultural Revolution. Among the survivors, Chen Yun, who was in his late seventies by the time, stood at the head of the line. He was a giant even among his peers. He had been a member of the politburo since 1937 and had headed the Party's Organization Department from 1937 to 1945 that put him in a position from which he could build his own support base. After the founding of the People's Republic of China, he became New China's chief economic planner. He had progressive ideas in the 1950s and called for some use of market forces as a supplement to the planned economy.[4] It was Chen Yun who led the efforts to pull the Chinese economy out of the catastrophic collapse that followed Mao's Great Leap Forward after 1962. It is also a measure of his political astuteness that he survived the Cultural Revolution largely untouched, even though he was out of power.

Chen Yun re-emerged as a leader equal in stature to Deng after 1978. Planning and control over the economic levers were his watchwords. Deng may have differed from him over specific policy, but both stood on the same side when it came to preventing the re-emergence of factional rivalry and ultra-leftism, or permitting ideas about democracy and Western capitalism to grow roots in

The supreme leader of the Chinese Communist Party, Deng Xiaoping (1907–97), after being reinstated as vice chairman of the Party's Central Committee on 22 September 1976.

Hu Yaobang (1915–89), the liberal leader whose death spurred the 1989 protests, was the general secretary of the Party from 1982 to 1987 before he was forced to resign.

Zhao Ziyang (1919–2005), third premier of China and general secretary of the Party, with student protesters in Beijing on 19 May 1989.

Li Peng (1928–2019), fourth premier of China, also known as the 'butcher of Beijing', addressing National People's Congress on 20 March 1990.

ELDERS OF THE COMMUNIST PARTY OF CHINA

Chen Yun (1905–95)

Li Xiannian (1909–92)

Yang Shangkun (1907–98)

Peng Zhen (1902–97)

Wang Zhen (1908–93)

Bo Yibo (1908–2007)

Deng Yingchao (1904–92)

China. With his power and influence secure, Chen Yun seemed content to play an economic role behind the scenes in 1984.

This formidable leader was flanked by others, all veterans of the civil war and survivors of the Cultural Revolution. They included Ye Jianying, Nie Rongzhen and Xu Xiangqian, the three surviving marshals of the People's Liberation Army (Deng's old comrade Marshal Liu Bocheng was no longer politically active); Peng Zhen, the former mayor of Beijing who had been an early target of Mao's during the Cultural Revolution; Wang Zhen, who had ruthlessly 'pacified' the Muslim-majority part of China known as Xinjiang (Hsinkiang);[5] Li Xiannian, the doyen of China's financial system; Yang Shangkun, China's president and Deng's deputy in the Central Military Commission; Bo Yibo; and, last but not the least, Deng Yingchao, the only female in the Group of Elders and the formidable widow of the late Zhou Enlai. By 1985, Deng was able to persuade some of them to leave party posts, but it was still work in progress, and the Elders could at any time assert authority by calling for an 'expanded' meeting of the politburo to which they invited themselves and pronounced on all policy.

This was the cast of principal actors who were to play their parts in the drama at Tiananmen Square.

:CHAPTER 3:

Storm Clouds on the Horizon

IN OCTOBER 1984, ON THE THIRTY-FIFTH ANNIVERSARY OF THE FOUNDING of the People's Republic of China, a grand military parade was held on the Avenue of Eternal Peace that runs through Tiananmen Square. Deng rode in an open military vehicle, revelling in his popularity and power, as the millions chanted 'Hello Deng'.

Even as all of China and the world feted Deng, there were signs on the horizon that all was not well. The economy was still in positive territory, but underlying concerns were becoming visible. By early 1985 the rural boom which was sparked by the agricultural sector reforms was reaching its peak, but no additional gains were being made in the cities. Industrial overheating was beginning to take place due to government's spending policies in infrastructure. Double-digit inflation was recorded. Predictably, the government had resorted to tightening credit policies, but that, in turn, was causing a severe growth slump.[1] In these conditions, Hu and Zhao proposed to start urban reforms, beginning with price adjustment to reflect true market value. Discussions within the Party on urban reforms, especially on price-and-wage reforms, became contentious. The economic planners led by Chen Yun began to question the economic line. Deng, who was determined to pursue the Four Modernizations policy, remained convinced that urban reform was necessary. Fissures began to emerge inside the Party as the consensus on reform began to fracture.

These early signs were missed by the outside world. It was the beginning of the end of the Cold War. US president Ronald Reagan, the ultimate cold warrior, was engaged in the deepening of strategic cooperation between Beijing and Washington against Moscow, and would likely have pushed away any contrarian voices that sought to flag problems inside China. In London, another Cold War stalwart, Prime Minister Margaret Thatcher, was negotiating with Deng over the future of Hong Kong, Britain's economic lifeline in Asia, and would not have allowed anything to distract Britain from that negotiation. Prime Minister Yasuhiro Nakasone was leading Japan to an unprecedented period of post-war prosperity on the back of the Chinese market and Japanese investments in China. In Tokyo an entire cottage industry of politicians, diplomats and media barons had sprouted, who vied with each other to ingratiate themselves with the Chinese. Love of profit and dislike of the Soviet-backed Vietnamese puppet regime in Cambodia endeared China to Prime Minister Lee Kwan Yew of Singapore, who became an ardent spokesperson for Deng, while Prime Minister Mahathir bin Mohamad of Malaysia and others in South-East Asia were happy to ride on the back of the Chinese tiger all the way to the bank. As for the Europeans, China was simply an emerging market and they were content to leave the politics and foreign policy to Reagan and Thatcher. In India, where Rajiv Gandhi had assumed office since November 1984, the initial priority was to repair relations with the United States. In short, everybody who might have noted the situation developing inside China was distracted.

Deng publicly signalled his support for the Hu–Zhao line on economic reform in well-publicized conversations with foreign leaders from October 1984 through to July 1985. He told President Maumoon Abdul Gayoom of the Maldives in October 1984 that reform in the cities was complicated, and some problems may arise in the process, 'but it doesn't matter'.[2] He told Vice President Ali Hassan Mwinyi of Tanzania on 15 April 1985 that 'urban reform is more complicated and risky ... although some problems have arisen in the process, we are confident we can handle them'.[3] He delivered the same message to the Party Central Committee on 11 July 1985, saying that 'price reform will be the hardest nut to crack, but we have to crack it. If we don't, there will be no foundation for sustained development.'[4] Deng wanted to show that he was prepared to take the risk and stay the course.

On the opposite side, it fell to Chen Yun to hold up the flag of the 'planned economy'. Chen Yun was a formidable leader. Like Deng, he was in Mao's inner circle in the 1950s. Like Deng, he had survived the Cultural Revolution. He was one of the main proposers for Deng's rehabilitation and reinstatement in 1977, and, thus, perhaps the only one who could speak to Deng as equal. Therefore, in his speech to the party conference in September 1985, Chen Yun did not mince his words: 'We are communists. Our goal is to build socialism.' While endorsing structural reforms, he talked of 'the planned economy's primacy and the subordinate role of market regulation as still necessary'. And to make his meaning amply clear, he added, 'Guidance planning is not the same as market regulation. Market regulation involves no planning, blindly allowing supply and demand to determine production.'[5] The message could not have been not lost on Deng.

Deng was not to be deterred. His main goal was to proceed with his plans for leadership changes at the party conference (Fifth Plenary Session of the Twelfth Central Committee) in September 1985, and to bring up the 'third echelon' of leaders. He said as much to the president of the Japanese Upper House on 31 July 1985,[6] whom he met in Beidaihe (the summer beach resort where communist leaders traditionally gather each July and August for unofficial networking). At the party conference he was able to 'persuade' several veterans, including Wang Zhen, Ye Jianying, Nie Rongzhen and Zhou Enlai's widow Deng Yingchao, to leave the politburo, but Deng was not yet able to drop hard-line ideologues like Hu Qiaomu and Deng Liqun from party positions. Nevertheless, younger leaders like Li Peng, Qiao Shi and Hu Qili made their way into the politburo, and the transition was smooth. There was nothing to suggest a gathering storm.

It is not clear when Deng first began to harbour doubts about his protégé Hu Yaobang's political ambitions. It might even have been before the party conference of September 1985. Deng had backed Hu Yaobang on political and ideological issues from his early days as general secretary, when powerful conservatives within the Party tried to regain control of the ideological line by stirring up another 'anti-rightist' campaign against so-called bourgeois liberal intellectuals. Deng recognized that such a campaign might potentially derail his reform and opening China up to the outside world. As early as in 1981, when a draft resolution was being discussed on 'Certain Questions in the History of the Party since the Founding of the People's Republic of China', he had warded off the threat by telling the Central Committee on 23 June 1981: 'There are some other questions. For instance, when we analyse the causes of the Cultural Revolution, should we mention the influence of petty-bourgeois ideology? I think it does no harm to omit that reference. If and when it becomes necessary to counter the influence of petty-bourgeois ideology, we can deal with it in future. There is no hurry. That is not the question involved here.'[7] Deng's fear was that left-leaning ideologues might reverse the course of reform and modernization set in 1978.

Deng had fair reasons for such a concern. Two 'leftists' held key offices in the Party. Hu Qiaomu, Mao Zedong's erstwhile secretary, headed the Party's Propaganda Department and Deng Liqun, known as 'Little Deng' to differentiate him from Deng Xiaoping, headed the Party's Policy Research Office from 1982 onwards. They enjoyed the patronage of the Elders who wanted to keep checks and balances on Deng's power. The two initiated an 'anti-bourgeois liberalization' campaign; an ideological battle against what they called Western 'spiritual pollution'. These were all-encompassing phrases that might loosely be defined as the promotion of liberal ideas of any kind that would lead to the establishment of Western-style capitalist democracy and spell the demise of the Chinese Communist Party. In its place they called for the building of a 'socialist spiritual civilization'.

Through 1982 and 1983 Hu Qiaomu and Deng Liqun had railed against bourgeois liberalization as a tendency that demanded China forsake the socialist road and install a capitalist liberal system to 'weaken, eliminate or undermine Party leadership',[8] as Hu Qiaomu put it in February 1982. Deng tolerated this in the larger interest of seeing his reforms through, including his succession plans, but when Hu Yaobang's confrontational tactics, such as his open encouragement to liberal intellectuals to debate political reforms, began to threaten the Party's unity, he gradually lost confidence in Hu Yaobang's political judgement. Perhaps Deng sensed that China might slip into another Cultural Revolution if the ideological chasm became unbridgeable.

By the end of 1985, it was beginning to look that way. Two contending schools of thought emerged. Hu Qiaomu took the position that intellectual output of any sort, from art to literature, should be assessed not merely on artistic form but principally on its ideological merit. Hu Yaobang, on the other hand, felt that intellectual freedom should not be bridled so, and he defended the rights of academics to publish controversial views. The two Hus entered into a direct confrontation.

If this was the only fight that Hu Yaobang intended to pick, matters might still have turned out differently. But by 1985 others also saw him as a problem. His unwillingness to accommodate senior leaders in matters of appointment was becoming a cause for concern. His promotion of Hu Qili and other Communist Youth League members to high positions was seen as an attempt at building a 'faction' inside the Party.[9] Hu's efforts to reform the military, even though backed by Deng, were opposed by none other than Marshal Ye Jianying, a veteran of the Long March and Deng's protector in 1976. There was a verbal altercation between Hu Yaobang and Chen Yun over the former's views on certain economic policies, and the Elder, who was in charge of economic matters, proceeded to reprimand him at a politburo meeting in March 1983.[10] Deng Liqun quickly ensured that this verbal reprimand that Chen Yun had delivered was duly publicized to the party rank and file. What might have circumstantially appeared as turf battles were, in fact, signs of growing political friction.

Hu Yaobang's anti-corruption campaign against the central military and party leaders and their families also caused worries. The children of the leadership, disregarding the Party's own guidelines about maintaining propriety and not misusing their status, were neck-deep in business. They seemed to have taken Deng's aphorism 'to be rich is glorious' rather literally and had thrown all caution to the winds. Hu's anti-corruption campaign was tantamount to challenging the rights and privileges of the Red Aristocracy. The Elders regarded themselves as the vanguard that had fought to establish communist supremacy in China.[11] Hu was stepping on very dangerous ground.

In these circumstances, the tension that was generated in the Party, as a result of Hu Yaobang's determination to allow freedom to intellectuals, came to a head when it came to ideas about political reform. For Deng this was a red line, which he had personally drawn when enunciating his Four Cardinal Principles in 1980. The principles had already clearly set down the permissible boundaries for political debate. Deng believed that the absolute leadership of the Party brooked no challenge or review;[12] Western-style democracy and bourgeois ideas were anathema to the Marxist supremacy. He said as much at two separate meetings with Taiwanese visitors in May and June 1985, 'Since the downfall of the Gang of Four an ideological trend has appeared that we call bourgeois liberalization. Its exponents worship "democracy" and "freedom" of the Western capitalist countries and reject socialism. This cannot be allowed ... The exponents of bourgeois liberalization who have violated state law must be dealt with severely.'[13] His public comments were perhaps intended to put Hu Yaobang on notice. After all, as general secretary, Hu was responsible for implementing the Four Cardinal Principles.

This had not been Deng's first warning to Hu Yaobang over this matter. Sometime in June 1984, Deng had tried to caution Hu Yaobang, through his ally Hu Qili, about his perceived partiality towards liberal political thinkers. Hu Yaobang had ignored it. After Deng's public comments to the Taiwanese visitors, he again used Hu Qili as a channel in July 1985, to caution Hu Yaobang about allowing himself to become a 'flag-bearer' for liberal intellectuals like Wang Ruowang and Liu Binyan, who were intent on questioning the supremacy of the Party.[14] Hu Yaobang, again, chose to disregard Deng's advice. By the end of 1985, Deng probably realized that he had been unable to deter his protégé from his goal of loosening the ideological drawstrings, and decided to switch tactics.

Deng decided to set the terms of the debate. In the summer of 1986, he told Japan's prime minister Yasuhiro Nakasone and Polish leader Wojciech Jaruzelski that by political reform he meant the separation of the Party from the government, the elimination of bureaucratism and the delegation of decision-making authority to lower levels.[15] Deng was now publicly defining the limits of political 'reform' with the aim of confining Hu Yaobang's political explorations within defined limits. Hu could not have missed the point, but again refused to heed the warning. Once that became apparent to Deng, there could be no doubt on which side of the battle lines Deng would stand. Hu may have been his chosen successor, but the Party's absolute dictatorship came above all else.

It is also around this time that rumours began to spread about Hu's attempts to 'persuade' Deng to demit his offices. It was credible enough to be picked up by the CIA and reported back to Washington. The CIA's assessment was that 'although frictions have been reported between Deng Xiaoping and his protégés over the scope and pace of political reforms, the disagreements appear to be differences in generational views and not fundamental policy splits'.[16] Even the CIA's assessment did not portend the coming storm. Zhao Ziyang also acknowledged the existence of such rumours, though he dismissed the story that it was Hu Yaobang who had asked Deng to go, as entirely apocryphal.[17] What lent credence to such a rumour was Deng's very public response in an interview with Mike Wallace of CBS TV, on the programme *60 Minutes*, on 2 September 1986. When asked if he intended to retire, Deng said that it was a difficult question. 'To be frank, I am trying to persuade people to let me retire at the Party's Thirteenth National Congress next year. But, so far, all I have heard is dissenting voices on all sides.' He was saying no and very publicly.

By the time the Sixth Plenary Meeting of the Central Committee was convened in Beijing on 28 September 1986, Deng probably realized that Hu continued to push the issue of political reform even after he had set the limits. When the meeting began to discuss the draft of the 'Resolution on Building a Socialist Spiritual Civilization', which contained the phrase 'bourgeois liberalization', Hu Yaobang dissimulated, saying that he had no clear-cut opinion on this matter and encouraged the participants to discuss it. If Deng needed any further convincing of Hu's defiance, this was it. He decided that Hu Yaobang's continuation in the position of the general secretary would be detrimental to the Party's long-term political interests.[18] In his secret memoirs, Zhao indicated that Deng tried to persuade Hu Yaobang to voluntarily relinquish his position. Hu apparently ignored Deng yet again.

Deng's style was typically to remain above the fray and weigh in on the issue as a final arbiter, if needed. But on this occasion, he decided he had to wade in. Deng called for a ten- to twenty-year-struggle against those who were seeking to introduce capitalism 'lock, stock and barrel' through means of bourgeois liberalization.[19] The Party's rank and file got the message that Hu had lost Deng's support. Deng had, albeit temporarily, made common cause with the conservatives because he now regarded Hu as a danger to political stability and the Communist Party. Many months later,

Deng was to tell President Mwinyi of Tanzania, on 8 March 1987, that there was a group within the Party which wanted Western-style democracy because 'actually Comrade Hu Yaobang shared their view ...'[20]

The stage was now set for the opening act of the drama known as the Tiananmen Square incident.

:CHAPTER 4:

Strong Winds

Throughout Chinese history the intellectual has always been the more respected and the more feared than the bearer of arms, and this was true for the Communist Party of China from its earliest times. Even before they came to power, while based in Yan'an in the early 1940s, the fledgling party, under Mao's direction, had carried out a purge against intellectuals who did not fall in line with Mao's directives.[1] They were labelled 'rightists', and the campaign against them was brutal, involving physical cruelties and mental torture. Some committed suicide. Mao was to use such campaigns time and again to maintain his hold on power – in 1957, 1962 and 1966. When Deng succeeded him, this weapon remained in the leader's arsenal. Both the shutting down of the Democracy Wall in 1980 and the anti-spiritual pollution campaign of 1983–84 were directed at the intellectual classes as a warning to desist from spawning ideas that, in any way, challenged the supremacy of the Party.

This did not seem to deter the determined few. Among them, three stood out in the 1980s for braving the adverse current of Deng's dictatorship after Wei Jingsheng went to prison in 1979.

The oldest of the three was Wang Ruowang. Wang had joined the Party even before the Long March, after being jailed by the Chiang Kai-shek regime at the age of sixteen. After joining the Party, he had endured several cycles of 'struggle' followed by expulsion from the Party. First in 1942 in Yan'an, then in 1957 when the 'Let a Hundred Flowers Bloom and Let a Hundred Schools of Thought Contend' campaign was followed by an anti-rightist campaign, and, finally, in 1966 when the Red Guards had imprisoned him in an ox-shed for four years. His spirit remained unbroken. During the brief political 'spring' in 1979,[2] he had supported Wei Jingsheng. In 1986, he published an essay titled, 'One Party Dictatorship Can Only Lead to Tyranny', which argued for public discussion between the citizens and their leaders.[3] The essay caught Deng's attention. Wang Ruowang once again became a person of interest.

Liu Binyan was the second of the three who would become a person of interest to state security. Like Wang Ruowang, he was purged as a 'rightist' in 1957, and like most intellectuals, he was exiled to a labour camp during the Cultural Revolution. In 1979 he re-emerged as a writer for the *People's Daily*. In 1985 he published the article, 'A Second Kind of Loyalty', in which Liu said that cadres should rely on their own conscience and not on the diktat of the Party. Inevitably, Liu Binyan became a marked man.

The triumvirate was completed by Fang Lizhi. An astrophysicist by profession, Fang, like Wang and Liu, was expelled from the Party as a 'rightist' in 1957 and sent to do manual labour in a coal mine during the Cultural Revolution. Following his rehabilitation, Fang Lizhi began to teach at the Chinese University of Science and Technology in Hefei, Anhui province, where he also began to share his political ideas. The 1980s were a heady period in China. There was political stability, the economy was growing and the situation was going back to normal, to the point at which intellectual questioning was becoming possible. The youth began to experience the power of education and knowledge, and to enjoy freedoms that had been denied since the early 1960s. Those who were in the universities in the mid-1980s had been spared the worst excesses of the Cultural Revolution, since they were children at the time, and the Party had thrown a veil of secrecy over the whole matter. The saga of the Democracy Wall in 1978–79 had been all too brief and quickly forgotten in a state that allowed no freedom to the press. Their ignorance of the past and their intellectual curiosity provided fertile ground for new political thought, and in the University of Science and Technology at Hefei, Professor Fang Lizhi was the catalyst.

Fang Lizhi spoke about his political ideas at a number of universities in 1986. He likely had Hu Yaobang's protection, and his speeches gained in boldness. He sought to test the ground for political discourse in November 1986, when he proposed to organize an academic conference along with Liu Binyan to record the true story of Mao's purge of intellectuals in 1957. Since there was no recorded history of that period, and many of its 'victims' had perished during the Cultural Revolution, the purpose was to preserve the remaining memories as a true record. Since all three academics were already under the scanner of the public security apparatus, their plan quickly came to the notice of the Party. The authorities mounted massive pressure on Liu Binyan. The conference was cancelled.[4]

Coincidentally, it was around the time that the idea of electing university student bodies was also gaining ground, but the authorities decided not to proceed with it at the Chinese University of Science and Technology in Hefei. This heavy-handed decision provided the kindling for the 1986 student protests. Whether Fang had anything to do with initiating the protest is debatable. He denied it till the very end. But the state saw him as a 'black hand'. The protests spread in a matter of days from Hefei to Wuhan, Kunming, Shenzhen and eventually to Shanghai by the middle of December 1986. Big-character posters calling for 'freedom' and 'democracy' appeared at the Jiao Tong and Fu Dan universities in Shanghai. These were elite universities in China's financial and commercial capital. Traffic was blocked along major bus routes. On 19 December, students forced their way into the office of the Shanghai Municipal Party Committee and demanded a meeting with Shanghai's party secretary, Jiang Zemin. According to declassified cables from the US embassy, university campuses in Beijing saw demonstrations from 22 December.[5]

Unbeknownst to the students, their protests coincided with the intensification of the political struggle inside the Party between General Secretary Hu Yaobang and the rest of the leadership. And the fight began to spill out into the open. On 17 November 1986, the *Beijing Review* published a report on a symposium that was held in Beijing on political structural reform,[6] containing two points of view – the majority opinion that political reform should aim to guarantee smooth development of economic reforms, which was the view that Deng adhered to, as well as the minority view that political reforms could be 'quite autonomous', because its objective was the 'construction of high-level democracy and not just at serving the economic reforms'. The fact that this was even reported was amazing because the publication of contrarian views would have been possible only with high-level political backing. On 15 December 1986, the *Beijing Review* went even further and carried an interview with Professor Fang Lizhi,[7] in which he virtually threw down a gauntlet to the Party's leadership by stating that the process of modernization in China was 'bound to involve a change in the concept of who leads in the political and economic fields'. He added, for good measure, as if to make his message even clearer, that it was necessary to create 'an atmosphere of democracy and freedom in the university ... there can be no doctrine that can hold a leading or guiding position in an a priori way'. The publication of his interview signalled that a political battle was under way.

Deng's task was a difficult one. There was no question any longer in his mind that Hu Yaobang had to go, but he had to engineer this without allowing the 'conservatives' in the Party to reverse the entire economic reform policy that he had laid out or permitting the 'leftists' to take over the Party. He also needed to pacify the students. He was fighting on many fronts. Faced with this conundrum, an apparent sense of paralysis appeared to grip the state. From the first student demonstrations in Hefei on 9 December, which continued till 22 December, no serious efforts were made to either address students' concerns or deal with the protests. The Party was undecided on what action to take. General Secretary Hu Yaobang was still in the saddle. But behind the scenes, Deng was already working hard on the political strategy and tactics to deal with the problem.

Deng understood that the public mood, if it turned against him, could still alter the political balance in Hu Yaobang's favour. Thus, with the students and the public, his tactic was to appeal to their good sense to preserve order and political stability, while making some tactical concessions on their grievances. In his reckoning, the average Chinese, who had grown exhausted by the mass campaigns and chaos of the Cultural Revolution, would support his call for political stability if he was seen to also be sympathetic to the students. On 23 December 1986, the *People's Daily* published an editorial, the highest form of public messaging in the Chinese communist system short of the Party's edicts, offering to conduct discussions on political reform 'through appropriate democratic channels', provided political stability and unity were maintained. Such an editorial would have had to have Deng's authorization. Since Deng had always said that reform of the political structure was a matter for the Party alone to decide, such an offer was, in itself, a tactical concession. In another *People's Daily* commentary a couple of days later, the Party even offered to put forward a practical plan for political reform in a finite time frame – one year. High officials from the State Education Commission were also asked to publicly convey that no action would be taken against students so long as they did not break the law. This forbearance on Deng's part was dictated by an acute realization that mishandling the protesters might unravel his larger game plan for China.

Deng utilized the time to align himself with the Elders and worked on the politburo to ensure that they would support him on the dismissal of Hu Yaobang. He was prepared for a temporary truce with the 'leftists' if it meant he could preserve the larger plans that he had for China. Deng was always clear-headed. His strategy was to tackle the immediate challenge first and then deal with the consequences.

By the end of December, Deng was reasonably confident that the student protests were being contained without attracting larger participation from society. He also concluded that Hu

Yaobang would be in no position to stage a counter-coup within the Party. Once all the elements were in place, Deng was ready to act.

On 30 December 1986, in a meeting with senior members of the Central Committee in Beijing, at which Hu Yaobang was also present, Deng signalled that he was ready to abandon his chosen successor. He directly attributed the student disturbances to Hu's 'failure over the past several years to take a firm, clear-cut stand against bourgeois liberalization'.[8] He identified Fang Lizhi, Wang Ruowang and Liu Binyan by name as troublemakers and demanded their expulsion, yet again, from the Party. 'Why do we keep people like him in the Party?' said Deng, declaring that Fang Lizhi did not sound like a Party member when he gave speeches. Referring to Wang Ruowang, he said, 'He should have been expelled long ago – why this delay?' He criticized Hu Yaobang for failing to distribute Deng's speech on combatting bourgeois liberalization, which he had made at the Central Committee plenum in September 1986, to the rank and file. 'I understand they were never disseminated throughout the Party,' said Deng. By saying this, Deng was calling him out in public as only Hu could have prevented its dissemination. Thus did Deng deliver the coup de grace to his once close comrade and ally, and now his political adversary.

Once Deng Xiaoping had clarified the 'political line', the state apparatus quickly swung into action. Vice minister of the State Education Commission, He Dongchang, held a press conference the same day, on 30 December,[9] declaring that the building of democracy and reform of the political system should only be carried out under the Party's leadership, and that this would take time, thus backtracking from a tactical offer which had been made in the *People's Daily* scarcely a week ago. He also said that only a small number of students had been excessive in their acts and opinions, thus giving an escape route to most students, professors and intellectuals, provided they resumed their studies and abjured further protests. The message was not lost on anybody. The public security authorities had begun arresting troublemakers. The country understood that the Party had united around a plan of action. The demonstrations tapered off.

With student demonstrations on the ebb, it was time to close the chapter on Hu Yaobang. On 4 January 1987, Deng summoned leaders to his residence to decide Hu's future in the Party.[10] Hu Yaobang was not invited. His fate was already sealed. Deng produced a resignation letter from Hu Yaobang and proposed that it be accepted. Nobody demurred. Deng was determined to make an example of Hu and he hinted as much to Takeshita Noboru, secretary general of Japan's Liberal Democratic Party, on 13 January 1987, when he said that calls for westernization and adoption of the capitalist system had come from inside the Communist Party. 'This time,' he said, 'we are going to make a point of checking upon discipline.'[11]

The conservative Elder Bo Yibo was asked to organize a 'life meeting'[12] of the Party from 10 to 15 January 1987 to criticize Hu Yaobang.[13] Such criticism and self-criticism sessions are common in communist China. They are intended to humiliate the subject(s) of the criticism sessions, and give them an opportunity to acknowledge their 'mistakes'. During Mao's time these sometimes ended up with the victims being maimed or killed. According to various accounts, the criticism mounted against Hu at the meeting was so filled with vituperation that it possibly alarmed Deng. He needed to control the process; he had witnessed at first hand, and personally, what happened when these criticism sessions went out of control during the Cultural Revolution. In order to contain the matter, Hu was, therefore, asked to make self-criticism and admit his mistakes, and persuaded to 'offer' his resignation. The next day, on 16 January 1987, the expanded politburo decided to 'accept his resignation' and appointed Zhao Ziyang as the acting general secretary. In a tersely worded communique, Hu was held responsible for violating the principle of collective responsibility and for mistakes on 'questions of political principles'. He was stripped of all party and government positions but was allowed to retain his seat on the politburo. Deng's hand was clearly visible here too. The Party did not need another witch-hunt, as during the Cultural Revolution, which could derail the Four Modernizations. On 20 January 1987, Deng told President Robert Mugabe of Zimbabwe that although Hu had been removed because he showed weak leadership during the student protests, his case 'has been handled reasonably, or quite gently, I should say, and it was settled very smoothly'.[14]

The dismissal of Hu Yaobang demonstrated clearly where Deng's sympathies lay on the question of Western-style political reform. Deng also demonstrated that he had a grip over the system. However, Western embassies felt that Deng's position had weakened as a result of Hu Yaobang's dismissal. One CIA assessment felt that conservatives like Chen Yun, Peng Zhen and Bo Yibo had 'forcefully reasserted' their influence.[15] This was wishful thinking. The assessment was correct, inasmuch as the conservatives were concerned, that the experimentation with market forces and the loosening of restraints on ideological debate might eventually lead to the undermining of the Party's grip on power, but Deng was still the supreme leader and remained unchallenged. However, the sense that Deng had weakened to a lesser or greater degree persisted in diplomatic circles in Beijing and elsewhere. More significantly, little weight was given by analysts to the role that public concerns over the economy, corruption in the Party and other grievances had played in the students' protests. This unidimensional view might have contributed to the misjudgement by the Western community of what happened in Tiananmen in the early summer of 1989.

Retribution came swiftly to those whom Hu Yaobang had backed. On 12 January 1987, Fang Lizhi was dismissed from his position of vice president of the Chinese University of Science and Technology and, subsequently, from the Party for advocating bourgeois liberalism, defaming the leadership, slandering the socialist system and sowing discord among Party members and younger intellectuals.[16] He was demoted to the post of a researcher and sent to the Beijing Observatory. A day later, on 13 January, Wang Ruowang was also expelled from the Party on similar charges,[17] and Liu Binyan, the third member of the triumvirate that Deng had referred to in his internal speech on 30 December, lost his membership to the Party on 24 January.[18] Deng meant every word of what he said to Chairman Arvo Aalto of the Communist Party of Finland on 15 January 1987 – that Chinese Marxists could not agree to bourgeois liberal ideology under any circumstances.[17]

So, the curtain came down on this brief episode. Deng cut loose his chosen successor who had become a liability. By placing all the responsibility on Hu alone (in Central Document Number Three issued by the Party on 19 January 1987), the presumption was closure. But while the immediate challenge had been tackled, the underlying contradictions were still in play. Key concerns remained unaddressed – including the mounting economic troubles and public concerns over corruption and nepotism. These issues had nothing to do with the power struggle within the Party. They related to the ordinary Chinese. The demonstrations in 1986 ought to have alerted the leadership to the fact that public discontent was like dry grass on which any spark might cause a fire. It did not. It was only a question of lighting the fuse.

:CHAPTER 5:

The Lull

Z HAO ZIYANG, THE NEW ACTING GENERAL SECRETARY, UNDERSTOOD the politics behind the ouster of Hu Yaobang, and quickly lined up behind Deng on political questions. On 29 January 1987, in one of his earliest speeches, he publicly pledged his support for Deng's Four Modernizations and the struggle against bourgeois liberalism. Zhao also gauged that with Hu gone, Deng wished to return to the economic agenda. This would involve countering the 'leftists' within the Party who thought they had gained ground with Hu's dismissal. Within days of Hu Yaobang's removal, Zhao and Deng Liqun sparred over Central Document Number Four titled, 'Notification of Several Problems Associated with the Present Campaign against Bourgeois Liberalism'. They presented diametrically different versions. Deng Liqun wanted to take the campaign into the economic, science and technology, and even the education sectors. Zhao Ziyang wanted to limit it strictly within the ambit of the Party. He was able to convince Deng that if the campaign went beyond the confines of the Party, the reforms would be endangered and might even be reversed. Adroitly securing Deng's prior consent before he formally put it to the Party Secretariat, of which Deng Liqun was a member, he thus stymied the early challenge.[1]

The Zhao Ziyang–Deng Liqun rivalry played out over the summer of 1987. According to one report, Hu Qiaomu accused Zhao of acting like a 'money-minded merchant'.[2] Reports began to emerge in the Hong Kong media which, in the 1970s and 1980s, was not only a reliable source of information about what was happening inside China, but also a medium for selective leaks from top communist officials to send messages to the outside world. Zhao, it appears, had learnt from Hu's errors and was not about to repeat the same mistakes.

In late April he visited Deng and suggested that while the campaign against westernization was proceeding well inside the Party, it was being used by some people to oppose his reforms. Having obtained Deng's assent to check this trend, Zhao, according to the Hong Kong–based newspaper *Wen Wei Po*, delivered a scathing attack in mid-May 1987 on 'comrades' who tried to attack the reforms under the guise of ideological purity, and said that the drive against bourgeois liberalism was not tantamount to a Mao-style mass campaign.[3] The essence of Zhao's remarks appeared on the front page of the *People's Daily* on 17 May 1987, in an editorial, which said that to solve the problem of bourgeois liberalism 'we cannot rely on political movements, we must rely on positive education'. The same editorial asked 'comrades engaged in propaganda, theory, journalism and education to reflect' on why their campaign was not able to penetrate the minds of the people, suggesting that it was the shortcomings in propaganda work, rather than economic reform, that needed improving and rectification.

THE LULL

Since Hu Qiaomu and Deng Liqun were directly in charge of the Party's ideological and propaganda work, the targets of the *People's Daily* editorial were clear.

Hu Qiaomu and Deng Liqun pushed back by organizing ideology conferences in April and May 1987. Vice Premier Li Peng joined them. He was expecting to be elevated to the premiership and to the Politburo Standing Committee at the Thirteenth National Congress later that year, and decided it was time to show his political colours. His timing was perfect. He had pre-positioned himself as a natural foil to Zhao when the showdown happened. For Deng Liqun, however, the game was up. Deng Xiaoping had seen enough. In July 1987, Deng Xiaoping removed Little Deng as head of the Party Research Office (termed the 'headquarters' of the left-wing writers by Zhao), and Zhao presumably had a hand in ensuring that Little Deng was not 'elected' to the politburo at the Thirteenth National Congress of the Party in October 1987. This angered the Elders. Zhao recalls, 'They thought that I did what Hu Yaobang had thought about doing, but never did ...'[4] Li Xiannian, Wang Zhen and Hu Qiaomu openly criticized him. Since the Elders themselves were locked in a debate with Deng over continuing in official posts in the run-up to the Party congress, they may not have been in any position to challenge Zhao Ziyang immediately, but they chalked it up as a black mark against him.

It was in such circumstances that Zhao Ziyang made the error of opening up a second front. The sustainability of the reforms had already begun to come into question towards the end of 1986, and the student protests reflected wider public concerns. Such concerns continued to mount through 1987. Industrial overheating towards the end of 1986 had caused inflation which in turn led to credit tightening.[5] But Zhao Ziyang still wanted to press on with urban price reforms.

To be fair, the urban reforms were part of the 'Decision on the Reform of the Economic Structure', taken by the Party at its third plenum of the Twelfth Central Committee in October 1984. It had thus been endorsed personally by Deng and approved even by the economic conservatives. Its goal was to establish a 'socialist commodity economy', a novel idea, for which price reform was necessary. To that end, an important economic symposium had been convened at Moganshan in September 1984 to discuss the transition to price reform, and two contending schools of thought emerged. There were those who urged gradual reform of the dual pricing system in vogue at the time, in order to keep a control over prices and the economy. There was another group consisting of graduate students from the Chinese Academy of Social Sciences – which included Lou Jiwei, Wu Jinglian, Zhou Xiaochuan and Guo Shuqing, all of whom were later to rise to the very heights of China's financial system at the turn of the century – who submitted a report to the State Council (which Zhao headed as premier of the State Council) calling the dual-price policy fundamentally flawed, and instead urged comprehensive reforms. Zhao liked their idea, and in early 1986 set up the 'Office of Economic Reform Programme Design' within the State Council to implement the ideas.[6]

It ran up against the economic thinking of the planning lobby led by Chen Yun. Chen Yun continued to argue for a planned economy modified by some market-oriented policies. Chen Yun and the planning lobby, comprising Party veterans such as Yao Yilin and Song Ping, feared that Zhao's price reforms would cause the loss of Party's control over the economy. The subtext was the firmly held belief that if the economy moved rapidly towards market forces, it would seal the fate and future of the Party. Although the planning lobby did not seriously challenge Premier Zhao

THE LULL

Ziyang's economic policies in 1986 because they saw Hu Yaobang as the immediate threat, they thought they might be able to keep a check on him by positioning their man, Li Peng, as vice premier of the State Council, and ensure that their viewpoint did not go unrepresented.

With the entire leadership focussed on handling the Hu Yaobang affair, the economic crisis brewed unchecked throughout 1986. The reforms since 1984 had made no appreciable impact in the cities. On the contrary, it had created new problems. Commodity and energy prices had risen, and agricultural prices had collapsed. Farmers, as a result, preferred to slaughter their pigs rather than suffer the economic losses of bringing pork to the market, which, in turn, had created food shortages. At the same time, the prices of consumer goods began to rise because enterprise reform had permitted state-owned companies to sell their products above and beyond the state quotas at market prices. Faulty banking and credit policies exacerbated the situation. By mid-1987 the mounting inflation was a real worry.[7]

The state of the economy ought to have attracted Deng's attention, but he remained distracted with his unfinished political agenda. The Party was to meet at the Thirteenth National Congress at the end of 1987. He wanted to complete the leadership transition that he had begun in 1980, by ensuring the retirement of all the remaining Elders from formal positions of power and bringing in the new line of leadership. Again, economic policy fell victim to politics. Deng did finally prevail upon the remaining few Elders to exit the politburo and he too stepped aside, though he retained total control over the military (People's Liberation Army). Deng also saw his candidate, Zhao Ziyang, confirmed as the Party's general secretary. But the conservatives scored victories too – Li Peng became the new premier and Yao Yilin, one of the leading lights of the planning lobby, came in as executive vice premier.

While Deng was busy with the leadership transition, Vice Premier Li Peng and his deputy Yao Yilin spent the year 1987 systematically undermining Zhao's position on economic reforms. In the end, it all came down to price and wage reforms. Deng had, early on, recognized that price reforms were necessary and unavoidable, saying as much to leading members of the Central Committee on 11 July 1985, that 'price reform will be the hardest nut to crack, but we have to crack it. If we don't, there will be no foundation for sustained development.' However, it involved breaking a hallowed covenant of Maoism – the 'iron rice bowl'. Urban Chinese were guaranteed lifelong employment, and low housing and food costs. Zhao was proposing to abandon this long-held policy. It would involve deft political manoeuvring and sound economic management in the best of situations. China was not in the best of situations. The economy was overheating and price inflation was spiralling upwards.

Li Peng and Yao Yilin proposed that enterprise reforms, that is, changes in the way that state-owned companies operate, should precede price and wage reforms. When the Party congress anointed Li Peng as premier in succession to Zhao Ziyang towards the end of 1987, the conflict between the two over economic policy sharpened even further. Zhao was now the general secretary. In Deng's China, there was a division of responsibility between the general secretary, who was in overall charge of politics and ideology, and the premier of the State Council, who oversaw economic policy. But Zhao wanted to continue steering economic policy. Whether this was because the economic reforms had been his bailiwick for the past seven years or whether he wanted to deny space to Li Peng, the second most important leader in the formal power structure, is not known, but Zhao insisted on continuing as the head of the Central Leading Group on Finance and Economic Affairs. He claimed in his memoirs that this was Deng's idea. Li Peng was not pleased and he whittled away at Zhao's position.

The year 1988 was one of economic reckoning. Through the first half, Li Peng, now officially the premier, and Vice Premier Yao Yilin, both of whom had also been elevated to the Politburo Standing Committee, steadily accrued power in the State Council, undercutting Zhao's ability to steer the economy. Zhao complained in his memoir that Li Peng and Yao Yilin utilized the normal economic aberrations that happen in the course of any reform process to show his economic policy in poor light and to concentrate economic authority in their own hands.[8] The economic troubles began to spill out of the closet and seeped into the consciousness of party leadership. Inflation became a great worry. Prices of consumer goods and food went upwards through the year. Failure to raise the interest rates on deposits in tandem with inflation led to panic withdrawals and purchasing of white goods. The result was hyperinflation by the summer of 1988, running at over 20 per cent, and growing urban social distress.[9]

Party Elders saw this as an opportunity to finally cut Zhao to size. It was suggested that, as the general secretary, he could leave economic matters to the premier of the State Council. Zhao increasingly found himself hemmed in by the conservative economic ideologues and the Elders on the one hand and the new premier on the other.[10] But even as late as in May 1988, Deng still seemed to back Zhao's price reform proposals because he saw them as integral to his plan of economic transformation.

Every summer party bigwigs retire to the beach resort of Beidaihe. This is an annual pilgrimage since the days of Mao, where the leadership interacts informally in their villas along the coast, during the high summer when Beijing is unbearably hot and humid. These 'informal gatherings' were used to plot and scheme, and take soundings on the big questions, and even to take decisions that would, as a formality, be endorsed later by the Party or the state apparatus.

At the annual gathering in Beidaihe in July and August 1988, the economy was the elephant in the room, so to speak, and a discussion could no longer be avoided. A politburo meeting was held there from 15 to 18 August and a routinely worded communique was put out with a reference to price and wage reforms as key objectives of economic restructuring. But there were persistent rumours about serious differences in the politburo over this matter, so much so that Zhao Ziyang felt compelled to describe them as 'completely unfounded' when he met Shinji Sakai, president of Japan's Kyodo News Service, in Beidaihe on 16 August, with the politburo still in session.[11] Such a meeting was in itself highly unusual. His referring to the discussions inside the politburo even more so. It suggested that the differences were marked. In the next six weeks this tussle intensified and became public. It also became personal.

Premier Li Peng chaired a State Council meeting on 30 August 1988, where he declared that price and wage reforms will see no radical steps in 1989. He added that any further price increases would also be held off for the remainder of the year. Realizing that the run on the banks needed to be tackled, the State Council, under his direction, also passed orders that deposit rates should not fall below the rate of cost increases. This was entirely within his remit and in line with the politburo discussion, but it incensed Zhao who felt he was being undercut.

The serious differences over economic policy at Beidaihe finally appeared to have alerted Deng, who signalled his disquiet at a high-level review meeting on price and wage reforms on 12 September 1988. He repeatedly underscored the importance of staying united, saying that reform could be carried out only under unified central leadership and in an orderly fashion. But his position also took on a new nuance when he said, 'By reform, I mean not just reform of prices but comprehensive reform in all other areas also.'[12] He was evidently upset over the extent of Zhao's insistence on his own views about economic policy to the exclusion of all other views, and said as much by telling this meeting that if the State Council and the Central Committee had no authority on this matter, the situation could get out of control. Deng was prepared to lend his support to his protégés, but only up to the point that the unity of the Party and collective leadership remained intact. When these core principles were breached by Hu Yaobang, Deng had unhesitatingly abandoned him in the larger interest. Deng's words on 12 September were words of caution. Zhao should have seen the shifting sands. Perhaps he chose not to.

Just days later, on 19 September, General Secretary Zhao Ziyang told Nobel laureate Milton Freedman that pricing reform will be at the top of the agenda in 1989, though enterprise reform will also be carried out.[13] This was a cardinal error. The sequencing and priority of the reform that he shared with Freedman was in contradiction to what Li Peng had proclaimed on 30 August and what Deng had said on 12 September. Zhao's publicly enunciated views were tantamount to breaking party discipline and the principle of collective leadership. Deng had presumably had enough.

At the third plenum of the Thirteenth Party Conference, held in Beijing from 26 to 30 September, Zhao Ziyang was compelled to publicly reverse course. This would have undoubtedly been at Deng's behest. In his report to the conference, he was made to say that 'pricing reform is going to slow down next year, but reform of the enterprises shall be intensified'. In this manner, it was announced to China and the world that economic policy was no longer guided by him. In the ensuing communique of the Central Committee, the pride of place was given to enterprise reform, and in a final humiliation for Zhao, on 30 September Li Peng announced to the whole country, in the presence of the diplomatic corps, at the National Day reception in the Great Hall of the People, that China will put the brakes on an overheating economy and check further price rises. The general secretary had lost his battle over the economy to his rival Li Peng, and very publicly.

It must have been a very bitter pill to swallow. After all, Zhao Ziyang had not only done the first experiments in economic reform as the party secretary of Sichuan in 1975, but had also developed the national blueprint in 1980. China's visible economic achievements and progress were his to claim. Now he was being separated from the very process of determining the future direction of national economic policy. Stymied on the economic front, Zhao Ziyang decided to counterattack on the political front.

He started by permitting a meeting of intellectuals in December 1988 to commemorate the tenth anniversary of the reforms, at which several academics attacked the conservatives and the 'left-wing' in the Party.[14] One essay, in particular, by Su Shaozhi, was harsh. It was printed in full by the Shanghai-based *World Economic Herald*, whose editor, Qin Benli, was quickly emerging as a standard-bearer for liberal views. This could not have been done without the blessings of Zhao, since the Propaganda Department was within Zhao's portfolio. The Elders were upset. In early 1989, Chen Yun reportedly circulated his 'Eight Opinions', accusing Zhao Ziyang of falling short on ideological and propaganda work. Other leaders also petitioned Deng to close down the *World Economic Herald* and ask Zhao to perform self-criticism.[15] The Hong Kong media claimed that by March 1989, Li Xiannian was even urging Deng to ask for Zhao's resignation. Opposition to Zhao mounted through early 1989.

It was around this time that Fang Lizhi re-emerged from relative obscurity as a researcher at the Beijing Observatory, to pose a problem for Deng. On 6 January 1989, he wrote an open letter to Deng seeking the release of all political prisoners in China, especially Wei Jingsheng. After Fang's demotion and transfer to an inconsequential position in Beijing in early 1987, he had suffered no further harm. He was even allowed to travel abroad although he remained under official scrutiny. While in Perth, Australia, in mid-1988, Fang Lizhi had made comments to the overseas Chinese students about Chinese leaders having foreign bank accounts. Fang claimed that this was not an original idea of his, but that he had seen it on some of the posters during the 1986 student protests. Deng took it as a personal attack and said he would sue Fang. He never followed through with the threat, but then Deng's intention may have been to create an intimidating effect on others.[16] In such circumstances, when Fang Lizhi was already in his sights, Deng would not have taken kindly to the publication of Fang Lizhi's letter seeking the release of Wei Jingsheng and all other political prisoners on the occasion of the fortieth anniversary of the establishment of communist China.

The letter also came to the notice of the US ambassador in Beijing, Winston Lord, and his Chinese American spouse Bette Bao-Lord. Winston Lord had been an assistant to Henry Kissinger during his secret talks with Zhou Enlai to re-establish Sino-American relations in 1971. He considered himself a sinologist. His spouse, Bette, liked to hold soirees at the US ambassador's residence on Guanghua Lu, and invited artists, intellectuals and other 'dissident-types'.[17] In those days, Western embassies in Beijing were quite fond of doing so, believing that such patronage somehow helped in the promotion of human rights in China. In fact, the Chinese were contemptuous and privately amused. At any rate, Winston Lord decided that Fang Lizhi should be invited to a reception being hosted for President George H.W. Bush, who was making a state visit to China in the last week of February 1989.

Since inviting the so-called dissidents to such events was fairly routine in the Western embassies in Beijing, an invitation to Fang might not ordinarily have evoked strong reaction from the government were it not for the fact that this invitation came close on the heels of his open letter to Deng. Talk of democracy and freedoms by Chinese liberal intellectuals to foreigners was one thing; addressing a letter to Deng, who was officially retired, was an entirely different matter. When the Chinese learnt about Winston Lord's invitation to Fang Lizhi, it was received with cold anger in the Chinese Foreign Office. Lord recalled much later that when he had visited Beijing University sometime in 1988 to see the venue of a 'democracy salon', Deng had personally messaged his unhappiness.[18] Therefore, the ambassador presumably would have guessed that an invitation to Fang to a reception for the US president, at which Chinese leaders would be present, was likely to go down badly. And that's exactly what happened.

Lord claimed that the entire reception list had been shared with the Chinese in advance, as if this was by itself a great concession. The Chinese handled it in their own way. Vice Foreign Minister Zhu Qizhen invited Lord to the Foreign Office for a quiet word, and asked him to reconsider. Lord informed his authorities that the Chinese had done their bit by summoning him, and would turn a blind eye to Fang's presence provided he was seated in an inconsequential place. He clearly misread the Chinese. Vice Foreign Minister Zhu called him in again, this time when the president was already in mid-flight, to convey that if the Americans did not reconsider, Chinese president Yang Shangkun would not attend the reception. This set the cat among the pigeons. Besides that it would overshadow the US presidential visit itself was also the fact that this US president had served as the second US representative to China after the restoration of contacts in 1971. The refusal of the Chinese to attend a reception in Bush's honour in Beijing would play badly at home and spoil the president's mood.

Lord panicked and messaged the president on Air Force One. Bush was livid and gave Lord the cold shoulder when he landed at Beijing Capital Airport on 25 February 1989. Lord claimed that the White House had been consulted in advance. The White House let it be known privately that the embassy had made a mess. While the US side was locked in a discussion of 'what next', the Chinese did precisely what they do. They physically prevented Fang and his spouse from entering the reception, and the Chinese leadership attended it as if there was no cause for concern.

Much later, when the US State Department declassified their archives, Lord's contention was borne out. He had indeed sent a cable to the headquarters and the White House on 18 February, clearly conveying that the US embassy was planning to invite Fang Lizhi and his spouse, 'noted dissidents', to the reception, and asking for directions, failing which invitations would go out on 21 February.[19] Somebody in the president's staff had failed to understand the import of this telegram, but it was Ambassador Lord who became the fall guy. This was typical of the misjudgements by the Western embassies in reading Chinese intentions.

Deng received Bush on the morning of 26 February in the Great Hall of the People. The talk was mostly about the Soviet Union and Mikhail Gorbachev's expected visit to China that May, but towards the end of their conversation, at which many officials were present including Lord, Deng said: 'With regard to the problems confronting China, let me say to you that the overwhelming need is to maintain stability. Without stability everything will be gone, even accomplishments will be ruined. We hope our friends abroad can understand this point.'[20] Deng's message was clear. The United States should not interfere in China's internal matters if it valued the bilateral relationship. If the US embassy had expected anything after this statement by Deng other than that Fang would not be allowed to attend the reception, it had failed to read the Chinese mind. No damage control was done and denial of entry to Fang Lizhi became the story.

The incident had a greater impact on Sino-American relations than what could be perceived at the time. The suspicion that the US was seeking to meddle in China's affairs gained ground after this episode. It seems the Chinese anticipated that the US might cause further trouble, because on 4 March 1989 Deng told leading members of the Central Committee about his conversation with Bush. 'We have to send out the signal that China will tolerate no disturbances,' said Deng. 'China cannot allow people to demonstrate whenever they please, because if there is a demonstration 365 days a year, nothing can be accomplished and no foreign investment will come into the country."[21] Days later Zhao asked the Ministry of Public Security to establish units inside key campuses to monitor student activity, and the State Education Commission was asked to send work teams to prevent big-character posters. During the course of 1989, the future of the China-US relationship would hang in the balance because of Fang Lizhi.

:CHAPTER 6:

The Spark
(16–26 April 1989)

Saturday, 15 April 1989. The day began quietly. Winter was just giving way to spring. There were no signs of the impending storm that broke on the seven o'clock evening news bulletin. The death of Hu Yaobang was the leading story. He had suffered a heart attack during a politburo meeting, and had passed away at 7.53 a.m. that morning in hospital. According to his secretary, Deng appeared to be shocked. 'He immediately ground out his cigarette and crossed his hands weakly across his chest.'[1] The Party's official communique recalled his contribution to the 'liberation struggle', and in opposing the Gang of Four, as well as his work as the head of the Organization Department, rehabilitating thousands of cadres who had been victimized during the Cultural Revolution. There was no reference to his fall from power.

An embassy colleague who happened to be present in Beijing University that afternoon on some other business was the first to inform us about the appearance of big-character posters in praise of the deceased Hu. That evening students began to gather in small groups across campuses in China to discuss the news. The overwhelming sentiment was one of sympathy for one who they felt had been treated unfairly. The next morning, more small-character posters (*xiaozibao*) began to appear in campuses. Again, these were spontaneous, respectful and in the nature of tributes. Wreaths were prepared for laying at the base of the Monument of the People's Heroes, a stone column in front of the mausoleum of Mao Zedong in Tiananmen Square. Small groups of students were also seen visiting the square in spontaneous gestures of mourning. This conformed to the pattern of developments after the death of another beloved leader thirteen years ago – Premier Zhou Enlai. Those in the Indian embassy who were following this matter recognized that this was out of the ordinary, and we began to monitor the developments. If there were advocates inside the Party and government who were alarmed at this spontaneous show of grief, they were still in the minority. The leadership, as is customary, visited Hu's residence and condoled with the family. Deng was represented by his spouse, Zhuo Lin, and his son, Deng Pufang. Life continued as normal.

By 18 April, the number of students visiting the square swelled to tens of thousands. Aside from Beijing University, two other universities took a lead – the People's University (Renmin Daxue) and the Central Nationalities Institute. The base of the Monument to the People's Heroes was gradually almost entirely covered with paper wreaths, flowers and elegies to Hu, handwritten on paper and pasted to the column. A growing number of ordinary people were reading them. Criticism about the Party began to surface. There were reports of random acts of throwing of bottles or shoes at the public security forces. The Western media understood that there was a potentially important story to cover, and began to descend on Tiananmen Square. Despite predictions by Western media, such as ABC News' Todd Carrel that 'if history is a guide, they will crack down soon',[2] the authorities continued to exercise restraint.

In the week ahead the numbers continued to swell despite public warnings by Beijing city authorities. We noticed the appearance of a three-metre-tall portrait of Hu Yaobang in the square. The first sit-ins on the steps of the Great Hall of the People were seen. The broad sentiment remained sombre, one of mourning for Hu Yaobang, but the first calls for dialogue between students and the authorities to address their demands began to be heard. There were indications that the unfinished agenda of the 1986 student protests may be rearing its head.

The students' demands focussed on four main areas – greater education and job opportunities; the elimination of benefits to the children of cadres; greater responsiveness to the citizens' needs by the government; and some personal freedoms. Hu became a useful rallying point because he had been more sympathetic than others in 1986. Foreign diplomats who had visited Beijing University claimed to have seen some posters critical of Premier Li Peng, and even one about Deng's 'neo-authoritarian' tendencies. We were told that some of the posters also contained references to Abraham Lincoln, the US Declaration of Independence and even to Patrick Henry's famous 'give me liberty or give me death'.[3] Yet the students' concerns were overwhelmingly limited to their grievances. But the Western media started to create the impression that the students were seeking Western-style democracy. The Western media's initial efforts to define what was happening in the campuses in terms of their own reference points was the beginning of a fundamental misjudgement by Western governments about the nature of the student movement as well as the subsequent actions taken by the Chinese government. Many of them got it wrong from the outset.

On the night of 20 April, a group of students decided to stage a sit-in at the Xinhuamen, which is the ceremonial gate leading to the residences and offices of China's top leadership. The Xinhuamen is set into the ochre-coloured walls that surround the entire Forbidden City. In early April, the magnolia and forsythia that bloom along its southern facade make it particularly attractive in the drabness of the fading winter. After the 1949 Revolution, Mao had decided to appropriate this part of the Forbidden City. It was ironical that the communists, who had fought against imperialism and feudalism, had then decided to reside inside the very symbols of the state they had overthrown. But Mao was nothing if not a bundle of contradictions. He regarded himself as the true inheritor of Chinese imperial power, and had acted like an emperor. In the years after Mao's death, several leaders had moved their residences elsewhere, including Deng Xiaoping, but Zhongnanhai still remained the nerve centre of communist power. Therefore, a gathering of students in front of the gate made for a qualitatively new situation.

This time the police gathered at the Xinhua Gate in some strength. They broadcast warnings over the megaphone asking the students to return to their campuses. A Xinhua News Agency commentary also declared this to be an 'anti-party activity' and thus illegal. The commentary's appearance was the first concrete indication to us in the embassy that concerns were rising in the Party. Indirect references to the play of 'foreign hand' also attracted our attention. The Chinese leadership, since the days of Mao, were convinced that the West wanted to subvert the Communist Party of China through what the American diplomat John Foster Dulles had referred to as 'peaceful evolution' back in 1958.

I recall it raining exceptionally hard that night, which made it difficult for us to visit the place for a first-hand look. We learnt that many students left the area of the Xinhuamen, but a substantial number also began a sit-down into the early hours of 21 April. There are two versions of what transpired next. According to an official version, the students left the police with no choice but to evict them after they tried to 'storm the gate', and this eviction was carried out without force, by picking up the students and loading them into buses for the return journey to their hostels. According to the Xinhua News Agency, no student suffered injuries, though the security forces needed hospitalization because some students had thrown bottles and other objects at them. The students' version, which was the one that the Western media chose to carry, was rather different. They claimed that around 4.30 a.m. they had been surrounded, beaten with belts and kicked by jackboots, their pleas for mercy had been ignored, and they had been evicted forcefully. Student leader Wu'er Kaixi later claimed that about a thousand policemen and soldiers had brutally assaulted them, and several students had been injured.[4] It is difficult to establish the veracity of either account. Since the authorities had shown restraint till this point, we guessed that the extent of police action may have been deliberately exaggerated in order to get media attention. As time passed, it was clear that Wu'er Kaixi, for instance, could do or say anything for media attention.

Be that as it may, news of the Xinhuamen incident rapidly circulated in information-starved Beijing, and it attracted the attention of the intellectuals and academics who had also been at the forefront of the 1986 protests. This incident, in hindsight, became an important factor in the latter making common cause with the students. Several intellectuals with a liberal bias, including Yan Jiaqi and Bao Zunxin, wrote an open letter to the National People's Congress supporting the constitutional right of students to criticize the leadership.[5] Some of them had just participated in a forum to pay tribute to Hu Yaobang, and saw the Xinhuamen incident as the right opportunity to press their liberal viewpoint on the authorities. The coming together of the students and the dissident intellectuals was the first of many happenings along the way to the making of the Tiananmen Square incident.

If Hu Yaobang had lit the first match by dying, a second individual did so by publishing. His name was Qin Benli, a Shanghai-based journalist who, like Fang Lizhi and Wang Ruowang, had been purged in the anti-rightist campaign of 1957. Qin had gone on to establish a small newspaper in Shanghai in 1980, called the *World Economic Herald* (*Shijie Jingji Daobao*), and had begun to push the boundaries of press freedom. The newspaper was rumoured to enjoy, unofficially, the patronage of the liberal wing of the Communist Party of China and, some said, even of Zhao Ziyang. It must have had a patron for it to survive in 1980s China. It was well read among the elites of China, and also assiduously followed by the more serious embassies in Beijing.

The *World Economic Herald* and the *New Observer* (*Xin Guancha*) jointly decided to organize a forum in memory of Hu Yaobang in Beijing on 19 April. The forum's participants consisted of the usual liberal intellectuals, including Su Zhaoshi and Yan Jiaqi, but also some establishment figures like Mao's former secretary Li Rui. The central theme of many of their speeches was that Hu Yaobang had been wronged by the Party when he was dismissed as the general secretary in January 1987. Some demanded that a 'correct appraisal' of his work be done forthwith. References to democracy and press and intellectual freedom were also made. Again, the forum, while giving voice to liberal thinking, was hardly subversive in nature.

The forum might not have attracted much attention were it not for the fact that Qin Benli decided to print the proceedings in the next edition of his paper (Issue No. 439), due on 24 April. This came to the notice of Chen Zhili, the propaganda head of the Shanghai Municipal Government, via the Hong Kong media. She asked to see the final page proofs as was her right under law. These were shown, and she asked for editorial changes to be made. According to one account, the most offending passage was in Yan Jiaqi's speech, which contained critical references to the handling of the students who had gathered at Tiananmen Square since 16 April in memory of Hu Yaobang.[6] While it was the Public Security Bureau that had been the target of Yan Jiaqi's criticism, the article also appeared to indict the Communist Party of China by implication.

A 'negotiation' ensued between the *World Economic Herald* and the Party offices in Shanghai. It seems that while that was under way, some advance copies that had already been printed found their way outside, and were quickly replicated and pasted on university noticeboards. Clearly, this could not have been a coincidence. The secretary of the Shanghai Municipal Party Committee, Jiang Zemin, was unhappy by all accounts and demanded an explanation. Having survived the student protests of December 1986, he had more than an inkling of what might happen to him if he wavered. Jiang, therefore, insisted that Qin Benli must print a 'revised' text.[7] Qin Benli demurred, pointing out that in doing so the credibility of both the paper and the reputation of the Party would suffer, since advance copies were already circulating in public. Ultimately, the newspaper's 439th issue did not appear in print on its scheduled date – 24 April.

The reading public noticed that the paper had not been printed. It began to attract adverse comment. Even then it might not have become the cause célèbre that it did without the next steps taken by the local political dispensation. An already upset Jiang Zemin suspended Chief Editor Qin Benli and sent a work team from the Party to 'supervise' the *World Economic Herald*. Thus, a provincial affair known to a relatively small number of people was transformed into a national cause.

Qin's dismissal was seen as an assault on the Chinese media everywhere. A number of students on campuses who were privately unhappy that their marches to Tiananmen were not being covered in the media joined in the criticism of the actions of the Shanghai Municipal Committee. One poster seen on the Beijing University campus depicted a conversation between Cuban dictator Fidel Castro and French emperor Napoleon Bonaparte; Fidel tells Napoleon that if he had the People's Liberation Army to command he would never have lost the Battle of Waterloo, to which Napoleon responds that if he had the Chinese media with him nobody would have known of his defeat.[8] It was dark humour, but it summed up the feelings of frustration among students that nobody was paying any attention to their causes. Younger journalists, in particular those who had come of age in post-Cultural Revolution China and thus had only second-hand memories of those oppressive times, were also chafing over the manipulation of facts and censorship that the Party was exercising over the reporting on the student protests. Qin's dismissal outraged them as well. It was to lead the media to petition the Communist Party's propaganda bosses for press freedom by mid-May.[9] It is believed that even Zhao Ziyang, at a politburo meeting on 10 May, described Jiang Zemin's actions as 'hasty and careless'.[10] But if there was disquiet among Zhao or other leaders, nobody tried to get Jiang Zemin to reverse course. On 28 April, the *China Youth Daily* became the first to publicly telegraph its support to fellow journalists in the *World Economic Herald*, and a day later journalists from the *China Daily* followed suit. Each action that the Communist Party of China took appeared to draw another constituency into the maelstrom, and so, bit by bit, the protests began to take on a larger hue. As for Qin himself, he disappeared from public view. He was placed under house arrest and never returned to the *World Economic Herald*.

Hu's funeral service was planned for 22 April. In China the funeral of a top leader is taken very seriously. It is a state event, stage-managed to allow the surviving leaders to pay formal respects to their dead colleague. It takes place in the Great Hall of the People, and since the entire top leadership is in attendance, the square is officially closed to the public for reasons of security. Although there were prohibitory orders in force, students began marching to Tiananmen Square, carrying banners and shouting slogans. They came from many educational institutions in the capital, including from Beijing University of Aeronautics and Astronautics, Beijing University of Agriculture and even from Nankai University in Tianjin. Beijing University carried a banner describing Hu Yaobang as 'China's soul', which was duly planted in the square. The security forces showed restraint, and did not block the marchers. It was clear that there was no decision from the top directing them to do that. The authorities had even made provision for those in the square to listen to the proceedings of the memorial service inside the Great Hall of the People.

In keeping with the solemnity of the occasion, the leadership was dressed appropriately in Mao suits. General Secretary Zhao Ziyang read out the eulogy. Deng looked ill and tired on television, but stood through the forty-minute event. The leaders then filed past the body lying in state. Deng did not appear to exchange any words with his widow. It had been decided that there would be no public viewing. The hearse lined up to take the mortal remains to the crematorium. In scenes reminiscent of Premier Zhou Enlai's funeral, citizens lined the streets to pay their last respects as the funeral cortege wound its way from the Great Hall of the

People and down the Avenue of Eternal Peace to the Ba Bao Shan Revolutionary Cemetery. According to Xinhua News Agency, over one million people had lined the funeral route.

As the leaders began to depart from the Great Hall of the People, another drama was unfolding in front of the ceremonial entrance. The young student leader, Wu'er Kaixi, Uighur by ethnicity and a minority in the Han Chinese–dominated state, who was studying at Beijing Normal University, used a bullhorn to stridently demand that Premier Li Peng must personally come out of the Great Hall of the People to receive a petition from the students. It was a bold and provocative act followed by an even more dramatic one. Three student leaders, Zhang Zhiyong, Guo Haifeng and Zhou Yongjun kneeled on the steps of the Great Hall of the People, and held the petition aloft, in the manner of supplicants before Chinese emperors in yesteryears. Nobody bothered to come out and fetch it. Perhaps the leadership may not have been aware of it at that point of time, but it was yet another indication that the Party was unable to read the public mood. Youth kneeling before power makes for powerful visual images. The Western media got their first big story. But what ought to have concerned the leadership more was that the very next day, on 23 April, a small Beijing newspaper, the *Science and Technology Daily*, became the first Chinese media outlet to break the silence by publishing a report and photos of the student protests.[11] It was now only a matter of time before the rest of the Chinese media followed.

Zhao Ziyang left on an official visit to North Korea the day after Hu Yaobang's memorial service. His absence from Beijing at such a time meant that his view would go unheard in a crucial Politburo Standing Committee meeting, which took place on 24 April 1989 under Li Peng's chairmanship, to review the situation. Zhao implied in his memoirs that his rival, Premier Li Peng, had seized the opportunity of his absence from Beijing to press his own views on Deng to take a hard line on tackling the student protests. (While bidding him farewell before he left for North Korea, Deng had told Zhao that he shared his assessment about the situation.) In hindsight, he should have stayed in the capital, but Zhao Ziyang had no means of knowing the direction the student protests would take in the coming days. He might have presumed that the befitting memorial service for Hu Yaobang in the Great Hall of the People would have satisfied the students, and that the protests would begin to ebb. A last-minute cancellation of his trip to Pyongyang might, on the other hand, signal nervousness and create the impression that the Party feared that worse was to follow. He apparently said so to Tian Jiyun, a politburo colleague, who had suggested that he reconsider: 'I've thought about that too; but to postpone a state visit would lead foreigners to speculate that our political situation is shaky.'[12] Besides, with Russian leader Mikhail Gorbachev due to visit in China in mid-May, his visit to North Korea, which was China's closest ally and over which China and the Soviet Union were locked in a battle for influence, was meant to reassure Kim Il Sung that any Sino-Soviet rapprochement was not intended to reduce Beijing's support for the North Korean regime.

Most of the students returned to their classes, but some began contemplating further courses of action.[13] Among them were the three students who had knelt on the steps of the Great Hall of the People. Feeling rebuffed by the refusal of the authorities to even accept their petition, they initiated the origins of an organization, in a small room in Beijing University the day after Hu's funeral, called the Beijing Students' Autonomous Federation (BSAF), and elected Zhou Yongjun as its first president.[14] Among their earliest decisions was a call to boycott classes. BSAF did not appear to have a very encouraging future as various universities in Beijing were already forming their own action committees. However, through informal contact and communication, the student leaderships of various universities agreed to BSAF's proposition to boycott classes on 24 April. There was very low student turnout in the classrooms and the boycott proved to be a success. We were also receiving information from foreign reporters that students from Beijing were travelling to other cities to coordinate activities. Although the funeral was over, we continued to see posters going up on walls and even on trees in the vicinity of Tiananmen and Dong Dan in memory of Hu Yaobang. The security forces continued to show great restraint – they were on standby, but seemed to be under orders to not respond to provocation. Violence was reported from a few pockets but no action was taken. The leadership remained undecided on what to do next.

On the same day Premier Li Peng, now the ranking member of the Politburo Standing Committee after Zhao's departure for North Korea, also busied himself on this matter. He was keeping a close eye on the developing situation through his State Council colleagues in charge of education (Li Tieying) and security (Luo Gan). He reportedly went to see Deng along with Yang Shangkun, and together they persuaded him to view the student demonstrations as organized, planned, premeditated and anti-Party. The incident at Xinhuamen in the early hours on 21 April, the boycott of classes after the memorial service, as well as the establishment of the Beijing Students' Autonomous Federation and their insistence on a dialogue with the government were all flagged as points of concern. Collectively, these were presented to Deng as a major threat to the supremacy of the Party. In the West, as in India, such student demands might have seemed natural and even reasonable. In China, anything that challenged the absolute dictatorship of the Party was unthinkable and 'counterrevolutionary'. In hindsight, one may argue with the response of the Party, but the developments that were taking place could no longer be ignored by a Leninist state.

Rumour had it that Li Peng finally swayed Deng by informing him that Deng himself was being vilified in some of the big-character posters.[15] According to one version, Li Peng claimed to have told Deng that the demonstrations had pointed the head of the spear at Deng, to which he replied, 'Saying I am the mastermind behind the scenes, is it?'[16] Li Peng was obviously aware that in both 1979 and 1988, when Deng had taken matters personally, he had resorted to tough action against both Wei Jingsheng and Fang Lizhi. It was, therefore, Deng who took the decision to declare the protests as 'counterrevolutionary turmoil', and authorized the publication of an editorial in the *People's Daily* to that effect. Zhao, who was in North Korea, telegraphed his concurrence. He later claimed that this had been conditional on there being no forceful action or violence against the students. If he had had misgivings over the editorial, he could have deployed various methods of reaching his concerns to Deng. He was, after all, the top Party official in the whole country. He cannot absolve himself of his own responsibility in misjudging the situation any more than his other colleagues in the Party high command.

The editorial in the *People's Daily* was to provide the spark that lit the fire. Deemed insensitive and unacceptable, it would anger the students, and what was merely a collection of people brought together by grief and hope would become a movement within the week.

:CHAPTER 7:

Conflagration
(26 April–9 May)

THE EDITORIAL APPEARED ON THE FRONT PAGE OF THE *PEOPLE'S DAILY* on 26 April 1989. It reverberated like a cannon shot. It was simultaneously carried by all major news dailies, including the *Liberation Army Daily*, which indicated to us in the embassy that the leadership had arrived at some decisions at last on the handling of the student protests. Titled 'It is necessary to take a clear-cut stand against the turmoil', the editorial in the *People's Daily* described the students protests as 'abnormal phenomena' and accused an 'extremely small number of people' of attacking the Party and state leaders and instigating the masses into breaking the law. The editorial called it a 'planned conspiracy' that threatened the country with a 'seriously chaotic state' if it went unchecked. A political line was drawn by describing the situation as a 'serious political struggle' and, especially, by labelling it as 'turmoil'.

On the same day, the heads of party committees in Beijing and Shanghai, the latter being Jiang Zemin, held study meetings to 'educate' cadres about the nature of this turmoil, and the police issued public notices banning further demonstrations without prior permission. Chinese sources claimed that Deng's name was invoked by the local leaderships. In his memoirs, Zhao claims that Deng was upset with Li Peng for making Deng's role in the decision-making public, but that did not change the fact that he had signed off on Li Peng's recommendation to take a hard line. The state-affiliated Beijing Students' Union also issued a notice declaring all other student organizations as 'illegal'. Police, and what looked like some People's Liberation Army units, were seen inside Tiananmen Square, a sign that the leadership was preparing to get tough.

Ordinary Chinese as well as the more serious members of the diplomatic corps immediately recognized that this was a turning point. It was well understood that such an editorial must have been sanctioned at the very highest levels. Speculation was rife on whether it had been done without the knowledge or consent of Zhao. Such speculation was largely the doing of the Western journalists, who had begun gathering in China for the historic visit of Gorbachev in mid-May, and saw this as too good a story to miss. They began to clutch at any straw they could lay their hands on in the hope of staying on top of a major story. Writing of a split at the top of the Party made for excellent copy. Few of them had any deep experience of China, fewer still a working knowledge of the Chinese language. Their sources were dubious, and often stray comments from random people in the square or speculation from the diplomatic corps served as material for stories. By the end of the whole sordid saga, the credibility of Western journalism would have been impugned were it not for the poor messaging by the Chinese after 4 June, which allowed for their version to go unchallenged and hence gain in credibility. It was not the first time, nor would it be the last time, that the

Chinese state and Party showed a singular lack of understanding about the free press and the democratic world, and the West would show a similar lack of understanding of Chinese politics and society.

The publication of the editorial in the *People's Daily* fundamentally changed the nature of the student protest and catapulted it into an entirely different trajectory. The infuriated students were galvanized to action. It energized the liberal intelligentsia. Chinese journalists, who were already upset over the removal of Qin Benli and the tight censorship on reporting, also saw this editorial as a further step in that direction. The unhappiness in different segments of society thus coalesced around strong opposition to the *People's Daily* editorial of 26 April.

Hu Yaobang, having served his purpose, quietly faded into the background.

The campuses in north Beijing became a churning sea of dissent. From the students' perspective, it was one thing to characterize the protests as a disruption, and entirely another to describe them as 'counterrevolutionary' and to allege a 'planned conspiracy'. They felt that their patriotism was now being questioned. The Chinese youth had always considered themselves to be uber patriotic, and upholding the banner of national pride since the anti-imperialist movement of 4 May 1919. Accusing them of being unpatriotic was guaranteed to rouse ire, and it breathed new life into the BSAF and the various university action committees. It also set off a serious tussle for leadership between the students. This was a problem that was to afflict the student movement from start to finish – the lack of a unified leadership.

Two student leaders emerged to the fore early on. They couldn't have been more different from each other. Wang Dan was a serious-minded history student at Beijing University with a reserved nature and, at first glance, did not have either the looks or the personality of a charismatic leader. However, what he lacked in appearance he more than made up for in perseverance. This showed as soon as he appeared before the foreign media for the first time at the end of April, impressing them with his cool demeanour and logical exposition. Wu'er Kaixi had, in contrast, a commanding presence and a voice to match. He was prone to sweeping statements and exaggeration, and frequently changed his mind, depending on what suited him. He had a low attention span and was never happier than when he was grandstanding before the world's media. These two became the two most recognizable faces of the student movement in its early days and they remained in the spotlight courtesy the Western media until the very end, thus claiming the two top spots on Beijing's most wanted list after 4 June.

Although the student protests gave the appearance of being well coordinated, in reality, they were anything but that. The BSAF itself went through several ups and downs in its first week of existence. Three presidents were elected and two deposed in quick succession due to internal politics. Decisions were taken and just as quickly rescinded. On 26 April, in response to the *People's Daily* editorial, the BSAF announced a march on Tiananmen the following day. Some people told them that such an act might be too provocative and dangerous, and was likely to invite forceful action from the state. Fearing for the safety of students, the BSAF president, Zhou Yongjun, on the advice of his advisory committee that included Wu'er Kaixi, sent out a cancellation notice. But the action committees in other universities decided to march on 27 April anyway, and simply ignored the BSAF's advice. It was Beijing University, China's most elite and famous institution of higher learning, which took the lead under Wang Dan. As they marched out of their campus, students from the neighbouring Qinghua and

Renmin universities also joined in, and as the marchers streamed past the gates of other universities more and more students began to march. Whenever the security forces blocked their path, they would simply sit down to reason with them, in much the same way that Gandhi had done in India a half-century ago – non-violent non-cooperation. As the numbers began to swell, we witnessed the residents of the city offering food, drink and cigarettes, and even intervening with the security forces to allow the marchers free passage. What had started as student protests were now threatening to take on a mass character, and it ought to have alarmed the leadership that the ordinary citizen was no longer in fear of the state. The security forces were faced with the dilemma of either using force against the citizenry or permitting the students to proceed, and opted for the latter. There were no attempts to block the demonstrations and no clashes were reported.

Soon the entire Avenue of Eternal Peace from the Jianguo Gate in the east to the Fuxing Gate in the west, a distance of perhaps ten kilometres, was a sea of humanity. Our own estimate ran into fifty thousand students, while others claimed there were easily over one hundred thousand. We saw posters calling for democracy and a new constitution, for the 'old to make way for the young and the new'. It was the greatest spontaneous mass gathering that Beijing had seen since the founding of communist China, and ironically it was at the same venue where millions had adoringly marched past Chairman Mao Zedong, holding the Little Red Book – a book of 267 aphorisms from the communist Chinese leader – aloft and shouting slogans such as 'Long live Mao'. Only this time, the Communist Party of China was not at the helm staging the whole affair; rather it was helplessly watching from inside Zhongnanhai.

The unprecedented success of the march by the students on 27 April electrified their leadership. It was too good an opportunity for Wu'er Kaixi to let pass and he promptly proceeded to oust Zhou Yongjun from the BSAF's presidency.[1] The ostensible reason was that Zhou had given the order to call off the protests on 27 April, even though Wu'er Kaixi too had been a party to that decision. But Wu'er Kaixi took the role of the president of BSAF for himself. Within days he and Wang Dan held their first press conference for the foreign media at the Shangri-La Hotel in Beijing, claiming that they were going 'underground' immediately thereafter because they feared for their lives. The Western media lapped it up. The students became the go-to source even for information on what was happening inside the highest levels of the Communist Party of China. It instantly transformed them into poster boys for a 'democracy movement' in China. A new phenomenon was just emerging in international media. It was called Cable News Network, better known as CNN. Mike Chinoy was the media representative in China and his coverage of the protests put Tiananmen Square and the student leaders, especially these two, centre stage as they beamed the news across the world.

The student leadership decided to draw up a list of new demands to present to the authorities. The principal demand was, naturally, for the retraction of the *People's Daily* editorial that had declared the student movement as counterrevolutionary. Demands were also made for an official dialogue with the authorities to redress their grievances, and for press freedom, including the reinstatement of Qin Benli as the chief editor of the *World Economic Herald*. The demands gained coverage inside China as the state-run media began to report more widely on the protests. Cracks in the system were beginning to surface. The senior leader in charge of propaganda, Hu Qili, admitted as much in a politburo meeting on 28 May, according to *The Tiananmen Papers*, which is based on internal documents and private interviews that two US scholars had done ten years after the Tiananmen Square incident. The same system, which a decade ago had been able to place a blanket of silence over the atrocities committed during the Cultural Revolution, as well as snuff out the nascent movement for more individual freedoms in 1980 by shutting down the Democracy Wall and jailing Wei Jingsheng, was now beginning to lose control of its propaganda machine.

The communist leadership did, however, sense that the editorial that they had authorized may have deepened the challenge they had on their hands. There was a feeble attempt at course correction while Zhao Ziyang was still in Pyongyang. The State Council, which Li Peng headed, said it would welcome a dialogue with the students, but in the typical two-steps-forward-one-step-back fashion they added that they would only speak to the 'legal' student union representatives. For the students that was out of the question. Nonetheless, a second editorial, milder in tone, appeared in the *People's Daily* on 29 April, titled 'Maintain the overall situation and stability'. According to one report, this was done at Li Peng's behest after he had been criticized by some Elders about what had happened.[2] Its purpose was to remind the general public of their fervent desire for stability and progress that was being threatened by this 'turmoil'. Only a handful of years had passed since the mayhem of the Cultural Revolution. Memories of that period were still fresh in the public mind. Such an approach had seemed to work in December 1986 and the leadership presumed it might work for them again. In a tactical concession, the 29 April editorial also clarified that the earlier editorial of 26 April referred only to a 'handful' of people who were engaged in disruptive activities. This was intended to pacify the student community by suggesting that the overwhelming majority of students was blameless. But there was no retraction of the earlier editorial. Deng remained firm on his decision on characterizing the situation as 'turmoil'. It was too little too late.

The government asked its spokesman, Yuan Mu, to engage with student representatives on 29 April. Accordingly, forty-five of them met the mayor of Beijing, Chen Xitong, along with Yuan Mu. In a further concession, the meeting was telecast live. Both were rather dour individuals, typical Chinese Communist Party apparatchiks, who used the occasion to lecture the students about their responsibilities and urged them to return to classes. Yuan Mu's arrogance came across on national television. It was a lost opportunity. It yielded nothing. It solved nothing. That was never the intention on the part of the authorities. Curiously, there were references to the role played by a 'foreign hand' and the Chinese Alliance for Democracy, a US-based NGO, in the riots. The leadership appeared to be toying with the idea of blaming the whole thing on the Americans, and testing the waters. This was confirmed after the publication of *The Tiananmen Papers* in 2001, which claimed that comments about foreign involvement came from Li Peng and Bo Yibo, among others. The activities of Beijing-based foreign media in the campuses and, in particular, their contacts with Fang Lizhi was also a subject of discussion at a politburo meeting on 28 April.[3]

Zhao Ziyang returned from North Korea on 30 April and immediately saw the seriousness of the situation. He also sized up the political space that it had opened up for him and quickly realized that if he could persuade the others to retract or reword the 26 April editorial, he would be seen publicly as a hero. From this point on, the students became pawns in his political game to regain the power he had lost since the winter of 1988. He called a politburo meeting on 1 May to try and put the responsibility for the protests on Li Peng's guidance to the leadership. According to reports, it was a heated meeting during which lines were drawn between Zhao Ziyang and Li Peng on the question of political reform.

Zhao Ziyang then tried to schedule an appointment with Deng through his secretary Wang Ruolin, but Deng was supposedly unwell. Zhao floated his idea to Yang Shangkun that a retraction of the 26 April editorial might pacify the students and avoid an escalation of the situation. Zhao knew that in the absence of direct access to Deng, his suggestion would reach him through Yang Shangkun. Such ways of messaging are common practice in the Chinese Communist Party since the days of Mao Zedong, who was generally inaccessible to all but a few in his circle. The message invariably reaches the ears of the leader, and his views are conveyed in the same roundabout manner. This system has the advantage of not allowing any decision to be directly attributed to the leader who, whenever a mistake is made, can conveniently lay the blame on others executing policy and deny any personal responsibility.

As anticipated, the message did reach Deng. A couple of days later, Yang Shangkun reverted with the advice that any modification or retraction of the editorial may not be possible. Yang said that this message had come from Deng's secretary, who also felt that Deng need not be disturbed as he was not feeling well.[4] Deng appeared to be following Mao's practice of keeping himself above the fray until it was clear on which side the scales had tilted in the political struggle. (In his secret memoirs, Zhao Ziyang claims that he believed the illness to be genuine.) In 1953, at the time of the first major leadership struggle within the Party between Liu Shaoqi and Zhou Enlai on one side and Gao Gang and Rao Shushi on the other, Mao had similarly retreated to Wuhan claiming illness, allowing both sides to believe that he would weigh in on their side until he could judge for himself which side was more dangerous for him. Mao initially allowed Gao Gang to whittle away at the authority of his deputy, Liu Shaoqi, to cut him down to size. But in December 1953, when Gao Gang sought the PLA's support to oust Liu and Zhou Enlai, Mao saw that the real threat to his power would come from Gao Gang, and he lost little time in destroying him.[5] Deng appeared to be taking a leaf out of Mao's book.

Although Zhao had not succeeded in getting Deng's support on his proposal, he was still the general secretary of the Communist Party and enjoyed huge power. Perhaps he took comfort from the fact that Deng was not explicitly against him and that he still held the balance of power inside the five-member Politburo Standing Committee. The Politburo Standing Committee is the most powerful organ of the Party and the final arbiter in all matters. In 1989 it consisted of five members – Zhao Ziyang and Hu Qili who were allies, Li Peng and Yao Yilin who were ranged against Zhao, and Qiao Shi, the security supremo who was seemingly neutral. Zhao also thought that the Elders might be in a state of confusion after the public response to the hard line taken by the Party, and unsure of the next steps. Zhao might also have presumed that the likely adverse impact of the student protests on the impending Sino-Soviet summit, which was to be Deng's big foreign policy achievement in 1989, would be playing on their minds, and the leadership would therefore be keen to resolve matters before 15 May. Zhao thus decided that this was the right time to reinsert himself into the politics of the crisis, and in the most public of ways. The circumstances certainly appeared to be in his favour in the first week of May 1989.

In communist China, public messaging can be done in two ways. One way is to leak information to the media, preferably to the Hong Kong or Taiwan press, but without attribution. Chinese leaders regularly resort to such tactics to air grievances or make a point to the top leader. The second way is to talk about it to foreign guests in the presence of Chinese media, so that it becomes a matter of public record and ties the hands of those in the top leadership who might hold contrary opinions. Zhao decided on the second path. The date he chose was 4 May 1989.

The date, 4 May, is of great symbolism in China. On that day, in 1919, thousands of students in Beijing had objected to the transfer of former German colonies in Shandong province of China to the Japanese Empire, under the Treaty of Versailles. Following great public support for the student movement, the Chinese government refused to sign the treaty although by then the Japanese had already taken possession of the former German concessions. Nothing changed on the ground, but it disillusioned many Chinese intellectuals about the West and created fertile ground for communism in China. Some of China's leading intellectuals like Chen Duxiu and Li Dazhao became founders of the Communist Party of China in 1921. Later, in the late 1930s, Mao Zedong appropriated the May Fourth Movement by declaring it as an early sign of a communist revolution in the making. It was declared a national holiday by the communist state. By 1989, which happened to be the seventieth anniversary, the May Fourth Movement had become one of the 'holy' days in the communist calendar.

Zhao Ziyang was aware that the students would march on 4 May. The so-called illegal student unions had already delivered an ultimatum to that effect if all their demands were not met by noon, 3 May. It also happened to be the day of a very important international meeting taking place in the Great Hall of People in Beijing. China was hosting the annual meeting of the board of governors of the Asian Development Bank. Many finance ministers had gathered in Beijing for this event. India's finance minister, S.B. Chavan, was also present. The dates for the meeting had been decided well in advance, and nobody could have anticipated the student protests in Beijing. It speaks to Zhao's political savvy that he decided to use his keynote address at this international event to speak about the happenings in Beijing.

The government spokesman, Yuan Mu, in a ham-fisted fashion, had rejected key student demands. The name of Fang Lizhi had also come up at Yuan Mu's press conference; he alluded to Fang's comments in the *Wall Street Journal Asia* – that foreign countries should put pressure on China – as a pointer to his role in fanning the unrest. It all played perfectly into General Secretary Zhao Ziyang's hands. He realized that students would come out in large numbers. He would have received police reports about the likelihood of protests in other cities, including Shanghai, Nanjing and Wuhan. By some accounts, Shanghai witnessed a demonstration almost as large as Beijing on 4 May. It was the perfect setting and the right time to send out a conciliatory public message. He saw this as political, as a means of gaining public support that might subsequently put him in an advantageous position vis-à-vis Li Peng or the Elders.

On 4 May, we were in the vicinity of the square to witness upwards of fifty thousand students on the march. They came from cities outside Beijing, from Shanghai, Nanjing, Dalian, Changchun and Jilin, and they were not afraid to advertise their places of origin or affiliation. The protests were taking on a national character. We also saw a contingent of media persons walking alongside students for the first time, calling for the reinstatement of Qin Benli. The loss of control over the propaganda organs was now becoming visible.

Zhao commenced his address to the assembled finance ministers and central bank chiefs by saying that, in his view, an overwhelming number of students were both 'satisfied and unsatisfied' with the Communist Party of China, but 'absolutely do not oppose our basic system'. The implication of this was clear: if the students did not oppose the communist system, how could their actions be described as counterrevolutionary? He then referred to their concerns over corruption, which he said he shared. This was also true since Zhao had spoken about this problem earlier, but on this occasion the reference was intended to win public sympathy. He then uttered the most consequential words: 'I believe that the situation will gradually normalize, China will not see any big "turmoil". This is my firm belief.'[6] It was Deng who had characterized the situation as 'turmoil'. Zhao was now very publicly reversing the leadership's assessment of the situation. It virtually amounted to a retraction of the 26 April editorial without saying as much, except that he was doing so unilaterally. Since there was no 'turmoil', as the *People's Daily* had called it, Zhao suggested that the situation called for 'calm, wisdom, restraint, order, a solution to the problem along the path of democracy and rule of law'. Without saying so explicitly, Zhao had also committed himself to the path of peaceful resolution and ruled out the use of force.

Zhao Ziyang later claimed that he had shown Premier Li Peng the draft of his remarks and obtained Deng's assent. If this is true, it is doubtful that Li would have agreed to it in that form. According to *The Tiananmen Papers*, the hardliners in the politburo wanted a condemnation of 'bourgeois liberalization', as a public repudiation of democracy and liberal thought. Zhao stuck to plan and avoided any direct response. He simply ran his speech past Li Peng in a perfunctory way more likely because his intention was to regain the political space that Li Peng had appropriated. His claim of Deng's support is also weak. Deng had time and again said that stability was paramount. He had acted against Wei Jingsheng and shut down the Democracy Wall in 1979 when it threatened stability. He had voiced his support for the anti-bourgeois-liberalization movement whenever he felt that Western ideas might be gaining ground to threaten the Communist Party of China. Deng had gone so far as to sacrifice his own man, Hu Yaobang, when he had become a problem for the Party. It is hardly likely that he would have given his concurrence to Zhao to reverse the Party line on the student protests in such a manner. It was simply not in character.

Zhao's comments on 4 May were duly publicized in the media, including on the front page of the *People's Daily* the following morning. Everybody in China read it. The foreign media ensured that it got huge international publicity. A Beijing Spring appeared to be unfolding. The students were euphoric, believing that the leadership was finally responding to their grievances and thinking that this would lead to the dialogue they wanted with the government. This is precisely what Zhao Ziyang had intended. After the Tiananmen Square incident was crushed, the new general secretary Jiang Zemin admitted as much to a visiting East German politburo member, Gunther Schabowski, 'With his speech to the representatives of the ADB on 4 May, Zhao Ziyang lit the fire again when the unrest had already become weaker.'[7] This would become one of the main charges against him when his case was later investigated by the Central Committee.

It looked like Zhao was making common cause with the students, including on issues that he had spoken of within the Party – corruption, nepotism, economic reform and so on. Nothing could have been further from the truth. When Zhao Ziyang referred to democracy as a means of resolving matters, he was not referring to Western-style democracy. Zhao was no democrat. He was a communist still smarting from the bruising fight over economic policy that he had lost at the end of 1988, and in search of restoring his political authority which he felt was being whittled away by the old guard. Democracy was a weapon to be used in his inner-party fight. If it fitted in with the narrative that the Western media had built, of a Beijing Spring where the breeze of democracy and human freedom was blowing away the cobwebs of communism, so much the better for Zhao. His remarks to the ADB board of governors had obviously been made with an eye to the Western media. And if *The Tiananmen Papers* are to be believed, reports on foreign media reactions to his speech which reached the Party headquarters, validated Zhao's tactics. The general line in the foreign press was that his speech would strengthen his hand in leading the Party towards deeper political reform. The foreign press in Beijing chased the wrong story. It was not a democratic revolution that was under way. It was a power struggle, and its outcome would have a profound impact on China. Not even Liu Binyan's opinion piece in the *New York Times* on 9 May,[8] stating that 'a high-level power struggle' was under way, and that a 'small power vacuum' had appeared as a result of the stand-off, threw the Western media off their belief that China was about to change its political system.

Having achieved his initial objective, Zhao prepared to use the Chinese media to expand his political space even further. Chinese journalists had been chafing at the press restrictions since Hu Yaobang's funeral. Outliers like the *Science and Technology Daily* and *China Women's Daily* had given some coverage to the student protests, but in a largely factual way. Qin Benli's dismissal had provided the younger journalists with both a mascot and a cause, but the senior management had still tried to steer clear of the younger lot and keep to the Party line. Over time, the journalists who had covered the student protests as well as the student–government dialogues, at the end of April and in early May, could not remain unaffected by the situation. There were sightings of young reporters posting big-character posters critical of media controls inside the corridors of the *People's Daily*. The fact that some of them were not immediately pulled down also showed some level of sympathy among the senior staff. It was just a matter of time before the media turned the corner. Zhao intended to hasten that process.

On 6 May, Zhao summoned Hu Qili, his ally on the Politburo Standing Committee, and Rui Xingwen, who was in charge of all propaganda activities, in the Party Secretariat, and suggested that there was no big risk in relaxing some of the press controls. Zhao asked Hu Qili to directly engage with the Chinese media organizations and convey his instructions.[9] It was highly unusual for a member of the Politburo Standing Committee to do this. Zhao's intention was clearly meant to bring him advantage in the inner-party struggle by securing the loyalty of propaganda organs through a nominal assuaging of the media's concerns. Control the tools for propaganda, and you control the population. The Chinese media drew encouragement and, on 9 May, in a remarkable act of defiance, 1,013 journalists from thirty media units presented a petition to the All-China Journalists Association demanding a relaxation of state censorship of news.

Luck seemed to favour Zhao Ziyang. His conciliatory speech on 4 May appeared to be working. The students seemed to be taking solace from the fact that someone high up was listening. From 7 May onwards, the student protests appeared to lose steam. Classes resumed on several campuses. The euphoria began to fade. Disagreement developed in the ad hoc student bodies over tactics on the way forward. In the 1995 film, *The Gate of Heavenly Peace*, in which many of the student leaders were interviewed, Wang Dan said that the students were tired of the mass protests and should be allowed to resume classes, whereas another student leader, Chai

Ling, said that she had felt increasingly frustrated because of the perceived declining enthusiasm among students for further protest action. There was disarray in their leadership ranks.

This was also a time of confusion in the Party's leadership. Many leaders were reportedly upset at the stunt that Zhao had pulled on them, Deng included. But upper-most in Deng's mind was the upcoming visit of Mikhail Gorbachev, president of USSR, which would presage the complete normalization of Sino-Soviet relations. The tapering down of the mass protests after 6 May could have momentarily pushed his concerns over the domestic situation into the background. As for the other Elders, until Gorbachev had come and gone, probably nobody in the leadership wanted to be blamed for advocating or doing something that might blight such a historic summit. For this fleeting moment, there was effectively a temporary power vacuum at the top. The advantage in this situation lay with Zhao Ziyang.

This was Zhao Ziyang's opportunity to seize the initiative by addressing the students' grievances, which he had publicly offered to do on 4 May. Many of the demands were not of a political kind at all; rather they concerned with better conditions for study, more avenues of employment and corruption. They were also reflecting broader economic concerns, including overinflation and corruption, which were causes for public dissatisfaction. On this last point, Zhao himself had spoken at the Party's last plenum in November 1988 in clear terms: 'We should learn how to swim in the sea of commodity economy without being carried away by swirls of corruption. At present corruption among staff members of the Party and government departments – graft, bribes, extortion, profiteering and squandering public funds – is bitterly hated by the masses.'[10]

Zhao would later claim that that Li Peng had sabotaged all his suggestions, such as establishing a commission against corruption with real authority under the National People's Congress, 'that would independently accept reports and conduct investigations into the unlawful activities of families of senior Party leaders'.[11] He also said he had wanted public hearings on the auditing of major state-owned companies (these were usually headed by members of the Red Aristocracy). At a politburo meeting on 1 May, he claimed that he had proposed that the standing committee authorize the Central Discipline Inspection Commission (akin to India's Central Bureau of Investigation) to open an investigation on family members of leaders including his own children. There is also an uncorroborated report of his conversation with Yang Shangkun on 6 May about investigation into allegations of corruption by family members of high-ranking leaders, including his own family, and their surrendering their special privileges.[12] The real question is whether he had made these proposals out of a genuine wish to address corruption or merely because he saw investigation of family members as a means of keeping the communist bosses under check. It had been common practice since Mao's time to use anti-corruption enquiries as a tool for control. Zhao knew that no high-ranking leader was going to abandon the privileges they felt they had rightfully earned by fighting for the revolution, and this might have been his way of baiting them and keeping them on the back foot.

Zhao called for a meeting of the Politburo Standing Committee on 7 May to hear reports on the student movement. What he heard instead were strong words from the hardliners on how his talk to the ADB on 4 May had created confusion over the Party line. Corruption was discussed and Zhao again tried to steer the conversation to political reform, and indirectly in the direction of a reversal of the 26 April editorial without actually saying so. The meeting was inconclusive. He then decided to convene a meeting of the full politburo on 10 May in the expectation that he would get the approval to press ahead with an anti-corruption programme. He also criticized Jiang Zemin for his mishandling of the *World Economic Herald* incident. The politburo could not reach any agreement. Zhao was general secretary and could have used his authority better to insist on fundamental decisions, but he was busy playing to the gallery including the foreign press. On 8 May, at a meeting with the leader of the Turkish Social Democrats, Erdal Inonu, Zhao made references to political reform again.[13] He thought that the key to gaining the upper hand lay in external projection, but, in hindsight, what he should have done was to use his power within the politburo and Central Committee to meet public demands for change during the crucial days of 7–10 May. By misjudging the public mood, Zhao Ziyang failed to press home the advantage.

:CHAPTER 8:

The Blaze
(10–17 May)

I N BEIJING UNIVERSITY, A NUCLEUS OF THE PROTEST MOVEMENT REMAINED active but divided on the next steps through this brief hiatus, which ended on 10 May. On that day, in a spectacular demonstration, thousands of students rode bicycles down the Avenue of Eternal Peace. From our balcony overlooking the avenue, it appeared like a black-and-silver river running through the main street. The atmosphere was festive. Fraternization between them and the general public was evident. The authorities did not obstruct the bicycle rally in any serious manner. The students no longer bothered to hide their affiliations, and proudly carried flags displaying the universities they represented. It showed a step-by-step dismantling of the tight controls that the Communist Party of China had put in place since 1949, and the government appeared helpless to stem the rot.

A new star appeared on the firmament. Her name was Chai Ling and she was a graduate student at Beijing Normal University but spent considerable time at Beijing University where her spouse, Feng Congde, was a student leader. On 11 May, when the first posters calling for a hunger strike began to appear in what was known as the Triangle, the space in Beijing University where big- and small-character posters were displayed during this time, Chai Ling decided to use it as a pressure tactic on the other student leaders. Enthusiasm for a proposed hunger strike was low until she took the microphone in the evening of 11 May. What followed was high drama and tears. In an emotional speech, she appealed to the students to take up the cause through a hunger strike at Tiananmen Square. Her words electrified the listeners and energized the student movement. Many were to later claim that they were swayed but with no real understanding of what such an action entailed. Wang Dan and Wu'er Kaixi supported her, although the Beijing Students' Autonomous Federation had resolved against a hunger strike. Not for the last time, divisions within the ranks of the student leadership would influence the political fortunes of Zhao Ziyang.

The 'Hunger Strike Manifesto' was quickly drafted using Chai Ling's speech as reference. The manifesto's language sounded like emotional blackmail. Statements like 'Hunger strike is the last resort. It is also the resort we have to take. We are fighting for life with the spirit of death', and 'We are still kids, we are still kids. Mother China, please take a good look at your sons and daughters. Hunger is already destroying their youth. As death is approaching, would you be able to stand by untouched' in the manifesto were intended to generate sympathy. And it did. The Chinese, as a people, do not show emotion, but the underdog has always won sympathy. Initially, there were no more than a hundred volunteers. The secret lay in the timing. The hunger strike was scheduled to begin on 13 May in Tiananmen Square, just two days before Soviet president Gorbachev's arrival in Beijing. It is doubtful whether Chai Ling, let alone the students in general or the leadership in Zhongnanhai, or even the foreign press, had any idea how huge this would become.

During the summer months the traditional welcome ceremony for a visiting head of state is always held on the steps of the entrance to the Great Hall of the People that overlooks Tiananmen Square. It is filled with pomp and pageantry, and makes for good visual impact on domestic and international audiences. For the Chinese, protocol is a serious business, and appearances are sometimes more important than the substance during these summits. This particular summit had been a long time in the making. Since the Sino-Soviet split in 1963, the two fraternal communist parties had been bitter adversaries. Deng wanted normalization of ties in order to create space for China between the two superpowers – the US and the USSR. This was an idea that he had pursued with the same vigour as his other big ideas – the normalization of China-US relations and the recovery of Hong Kong and Taiwan. So important was this for Deng that it had dominated his conversation with President George H.W. Bush in February 1989. Deng had acknowledged that 'there are piles and piles of problems in the relationship between China and the Soviet Union,'[1] and he tried to assure Bush that the Sino-American relationship would not be affected at all if things improved with the Soviet Union. But he had also confirmed that Sino-Soviet normalization was on the cards. That Deng and the entire Chinese leadership regarded Gorbachev's visit as a turning point was also evident in what Zhao Ziyang had told Bush during his visit: 'His [Gorbachev's] meeting with Deng will be the high-level meeting. I will also meet him. This meeting will mean the establishment of party relations.'[2] For a communist state, fraternal relations with other communist or socialist parties ranks above state-to-state ties. During the visit of the first Soviet leader since Khrushchev, China wanted to showcase its achievements in order to remind them that despite every Soviet attempt to undermine the young Chinese communist state, they had prevailed and endured and emerged stronger. Instead, what was awaiting Gorbachev were images of a group of starving youth in the square, holding the mighty Chinese state and the Communist Party of China to ransom in the heart of the capital city. Deng reportedly told Yang Shangkun when they met on 11 May about the importance of maintaining order in the square during Gorbachev's visit. 'What do we look like if the square's a mess?'[3] Deng underscored this particularly to Zhao two days later when, for the first time since his return from North Korea, he had a face-to-face meeting with him. It was threatening to become a public humiliation for Deng.

Both sides of the political divide tried to persuade the strikers to leave the square. Yan Mingfu, the head of the United Front Work Department, began a dialogue with them on 14 May, and a real chance at resolution seemed possible. He drafted liberal intellectuals who supported the students, like Yan Jiaqi and Dai Qing, to help him appeal to the students to end the hunger strike. Zhao still held a few cards that might have resolved matters in time to convince Deng that his methods were better than those that the hardliners were advocating. But Zhao was more intent on playing politics inside the Party than on resolving the public's grievances, and perhaps the students had realized that. On 13 May, in defiance of Zhao's appeals to the students to resume their classes, more and more students came out in support of the hunger strike. In their speeches in the square, they voiced their unhappiness over the lack of government action on their demands. Intellectuals like Yan Jiaqi and Su Xiaokang also tried to talk sense into the government. Zhao Ziyang did not appear to comprehend that the ground was slipping from under his feet. He thought by appealing to their patriotism, they might allow the Sino-Soviet summit to proceed as scheduled. By then, however, the extreme faction had gained control over the student movement, with radical ideas of change and little patience to proceed in the manner that Zhao Ziyang was advocating. Zhao's indifference in addressing even the reasonable demands of the moderates contributed to the division in the student body and helped the radicals gain ground. And the radicals were rapidly coming to the conclusion that time was running out. In defiance of Zhao's direct appeal, they exhorted thousands of students to come to Tiananmen Square on 14 May. At that point, it was becoming clear to us that Zhao had lost ground with the protesters to the point where they simply ignored his appeals. Zhao admitted as much in his memoirs. He wrote, 'My plea was printed in all the major papers. However, the students did not respond to it at all; they proceeded regardless.' It showed how far removed Zhao was from the ground reality by mid-May.

A snowballing effect began to take place. For the first time, the intellectual and academic communities, always important elements in China, openly joined the students on their marches. We saw them holding banners of the Chinese Academy of Social Sciences and other such hallowed research entities that serviced the intellectual needs of the Communist Party of China. We saw Yan Jiaqi leading them on. We saw Bao Zunxin and Wang Luxiang and others carrying a big-character poster proclaiming 'China's Intellectual Circles'. Five hundred of Beijing University's faculty, including luminaries like Jin Kemu, Ji Xianlin and Tang Yijie, pillars of the establishment, wrote an open letter to the leadership to enter into a dialogue with the students. Ten prominent presidents and vice presidents of leading universities did likewise, and offered to act as intermediaries. The protests were gaining sympathy and support across the public spectrum, and the authorities had to go to great lengths to deny that workers from the Capital Iron and Steel Factory (*Shougang*), which was a jewel of the communist state, were also among the marchers.

The hardliners, like Chai Ling, made ever-increasing demands such as a live television broadcast of the dialogue with the authorities, which could obviously not be met. The talks with Yan Mingfu failed to achieve any outcome.[4] In the early morning of 15 May, the other side tried to persuade the students to return to the campuses. Li Ximing and Chen Xitong, the party secretary and mayor of Beijing, respectively, who were closely aligned to Li Peng and the hardliners, also failed in their attempts. It was on the eve of Gorbachev's visit that, for the first time, the Elders – Li Xiannian, Chen Yun, Peng Zhen and Wang Zhen, among others – separately met with Deng and exhorted him to act. Wang Zhen reportedly told Deng that there were two voices inside the Party, thus indirectly suggesting that Zhao was defying Deng and the Elders, and he urged Deng to 'come down hard on these students right now'.[5]

Wu'er Kaixi, whose views on the situation vacillated each day, and whose primary interest seemed to be his own projection, suddenly made a surprise proposal in the square to 'move aside', and let the official welcome ceremony for Gorbachev proceed as planned, in front of the Great Hall of the People. He had reportedly secured an assurance from somebody that there would be no reprisals if they withdrew. Chai Ling and the others refused. The separation between the hard-line group and the moderates who had led the student movement from the beginning was now complete.

On the day of Gorbachev's arrival, 15 May 1989, the entire square was filled with students on a hunger strike and a growing number of spectators, and public sympathy was mounting by the hour for the starving protesters. We noticed a large group of *People's Daily* journalists calling for a retraction of the 26 April editorial. Another jewel seemed to have fallen off the communist crown. A young Soviet diplomat recorded his memories about the extraordinary situation where the Soviet leader was driven from Beijing Capital Airport to the state guest house through back alleys. The formal welcome ceremony in the forecourt of the Great Hall of the People had to be cancelled, and a hastily assembled ceremony was held inside the Great Hall after Gorbachev was brought in from the rear entrance. En route the Soviet delegation could see slogans such as 'The USSR has Gorbachev. Whom do we have?'[6] Nothing describes the sense of helplessness better than the words spoken by Mikhail Gorbachev to Rajiv Gandhi, the prime minister of India, two months later. Speaking of his meeting with Deng, Gorbachev told Gandhi, 'At one of the moments of the main conversation with Deng Xiaoping, a group of students nearly got into the building. There were slogans like "Gorbachev, you are talking to the wrong man", and "58–85, a hint about my age and Deng Xiaoping's age".'[7] The first visit to China by a Soviet head of state since 1959 had been upstaged by striking students.

That evening, when we visited Tiananmen Square, the crowds seemed to have taken possession of the entire stretch from the Beijing International Hotel in the west to Xidan in the east. We saw slogans that openly criticized Deng. One of them went as follows: '1984 – welcome Deng; 1989 – Deng is muddled.' Another was openly accusatory: 'Xiaoping, you have made mistakes.' Yet another poster demanded to know the whereabouts of Premier Li Peng. We saw banners from the Central Party School, from the Foreign Affairs College, both well-respected institutions of the Chinese Communist Party. And there was not a single member of the uniformed security services to be seen anywhere near the square. We also saw glimpses of student extremism. Some of them had become heady with power, acting as if they controlled all movements into the square and forcing errant motorists to exit the area. The communist state appeared to be heading for a spectacular showdown in Tiananmen on global television.

On 16 May, Gorbachev met first Deng and then Zhao. Deng's conversation was entirely on Sino-Soviet relations. He gave a long historical account, mostly of the wrongs that Tsarist Russia and the Soviet Union had committed against China in the past. Then he uttered the historic words, 'As far as historical questions are concerned, I touched upon them in order to put an end to them. Let the wind blow away these questions. And after our meeting we will not return to this topic again. Let us consider that we expressed our opinions. Let us also consider that the past is over with.' To which Gorbachev responded, 'Good. Let's put an end to this.'[8] With those words, three decades of hostility officially ended and Sino-Soviet relations returned to the path of normality. For Deng it was a triumph. One that he had worked for since 1986, planning and executing it with the same finesse that he had shown a decade previously in normalizing ties with the United States. If Deng was upset at the student protests taking place outside the Great Hall, he never spoke about it with Gorbachev. He was determined that this would be his day and that tomorrow's headlines would proclaim his extraordinary achievement to the Chinese people.

That evening Gorbachev met Zhao Ziyang, who steered the conversation around to the happenings in Tiananmen Square and elsewhere. Gorbachev talked about political reforms in the USSR, and justified it by saying, 'He who falls behind loses – this was confirmed by our recent elections. But those who have turned to the people, sensed the necessity of changes, turned out to be capable of acting under the new conditions.' Zhao made it perfectly clear to Gorbachev that he did 'not intend to take things towards creation of a new party system, analogous to the one in the West, where parties replace each other in power'.[9] He told Gorbachev that no party was capable of replacing the Chinese Communist Party. Zhao's fight was not with the system, but with the distribution of power within that system. The West seemed to have misread Zhao. But it is a moot point whether anybody in the West was paying attention.

Zhao proceeded to drop a bombshell. He told Gorbachev that although Deng Xiaoping had, of his own volition, left the politburo and the Central Committee in 1987, 'all our party comrades know that they cannot do without his leadership, wisdom and experience. At the first plenum, elected by the Thirteenth Congress, a fairly important decision was made – that in all big questions we should turn to him as leader. This decision was not published but I am informing you about it today.'[10] Zhao had disclosed a purely party matter to a foreign leader. On an earlier occasion when, in 1958, Marshal Peng Dehuai had spoken of internal party affairs to Khrushchev, he had been peremptorily dismissed by Mao Zedong.

Even this disclosure might not have been disastrous had Zhao Ziyang not deliberately given publicity to his remarks. Xinhua News Agency led with the news that Deng was still overall in-charge of China and, therefore, still the leader who made the decisions on the most important issues. Since it is the practice for Xinhua to obtain prior clearance for all news concerning the leadership, its publication would have had to have authorization from Zhao or Hu Qili, the Politburo Standing Committee member who oversaw propaganda, and who was also present when Zhao met Gorbachev. On the surface, the statement appeared to give all the credit for normalization of Sino-Soviet relations to Deng, but the hidden intent of the statement would have been obvious to others. Zhao was publicly saying that Deng was responsible for the editorial of 26 April and for subsequent action, and absolving himself of responsibility. Gorbachev understood exactly what Zhao was doing and said as much two months later to Rajiv Gandhi. 'I got the impression,' said Gorbachev to Gandhi, 'that with his [Zhao's] statement, he sort of wanted to face Deng with the situation ... For poorly informed people, his statement looked like praise on the part of the general secretary addressed to Deng Xiaoping who formally does not hold the highest positions. But I thought there was some deep meaning behind this.'[11] In his memoirs, written ex post facto, Zhao gave a long explanation justifying his action as borne out of good intentions.[12] If Zhao was unable to fool Gorbachev, it is unlikely that he would have been able to pull the wool over Deng's eyes, and the two never met again after 1989.

The students and intellectuals considered this as open season on Deng and launched personal attacks. The following day, 17 May, a group of intellectuals issued a declaration referring to Deng as a 'dictator' and as 'an Emperor without a crown and an elderly senile character'.[13] Banners appeared in Tiananmen Square describing Deng as 'muddle-headed', and demanding that he come and talk to the students. 'Students are starving. What are your children doing Deng Xiaoping?' read one of the banners. Deng's humiliation was all the more profound because the massive loss of face that he suffered was broadcast around the world by the media that had gathered in Beijing to cover the historic summit. Deng's grand achievement and work of a decade, the full normalization of Sino-Soviet relations, became just another bit of news.

Discipline and order broke down to such a degree after seeing the government's helplessness at dealing with the strikers during

Gorbachev's visit that even government departments began to send out delegations in support of the students. Banners proclaiming them to be from the Ministry of Foreign Economic Relations and Trade, the Foreign Ministry and even other so-called democratic parties like the Jiusan Society and the China Democratic League, who were under the communist thumb under normal circumstances, sprang up in the square. Foreign diplomats and journalists were walking freely into the square and we could speak to anybody we liked. We had conversations with bank clerks, hotel waiters, department store workers and pensioners. They had different grievances, mostly economic, and very few were in favour of toppling the system, but they had all come together due to the insensitive way in which the Party was handling their concerns. There was a feeling that they were not being heard, and they were openly critical of everybody, not merely Deng and Li, but Zhao Ziyang too. It was mayhem.

In hindsight, 16 May was the day when Zhao Ziyang crossed the River Styx to his political demise. His desperate attempts to salvage the situation, by calling a meeting of the Politburo Standing Committee that evening to persuade his other colleagues to join him in issuing a statement to the students to end the hunger strike, was met with open hostility from Premier Li Peng and Vice Premier Yao Yilin. His proposal for a revision of the 26 April editorial was rejected by Li Peng with the words: 'These are Deng's original words and cannot be modified.'[14] Zhao finally issued an appeal to the students to end the hunger strike. Nobody cared what he thought by then. The tide of public opinion had also turned against Zhao. He had lost his gamble.

The *Beijing Review* estimated that 1.5 million people were on the streets on 17 May 1989. The workers marched with the students. The media marched with the students. Even officialdom and the party rank and file marched with the students. Banners in the square demanded resignations from Deng and Li Peng. A banner held aloft by the Communications Research Institute read, 'We want freedom more than bread.' The China Youth Political Institute carried a banner saying, 'Democracy and law are guarantees for social stability. Dictatorship and corruption are the roots of social turbulence.' The Central Nationalities Institute walked under the banner, 'Fifty-six nationalities call for democracy.' Across China the people marched in sympathy and support of the hunger strike.

The wailing sound of ambulance sirens filled the air. Television cameras in the square beamed dramatic pictures of mass rallies and the hunger strikers to domestic and foreign audiences. Wu'er Kaixi dramatically fainted from hunger for the benefit of television viewers, and according to the French newspaper *Le Figaro*, he also declared that he was ready to lay down his life. In reality, Wu'er Kaixi was eating on the sly. On at least one occasion, he asked John Pomfret of the Associated Press to buy him a meal when he was supposedly on hunger strike.[15] It speaks also to the lack of journalistic ethics of some of the Western media that they chose not to publish this even when they were aware of it. Their reporting was selective and biased.

The Communist Party of China appeared to have lost control over the cities. Those who had a superficial understanding of events based on media reporting from China might hardly be blamed for assuming that a 'democratic revolution' was in the making, but when the resident foreign media and some members of the diplomatic corps encouraged this sort of thinking, it was possibly motivated. Zhao Ziyang's belated efforts at showing his concern by visiting the hunger strikers in hospital was ignored at the Hunger Strike Headquarters in the square. He was already irrelevant.

Deng's anger at the way in which Zhao had shown him in poor light in front of the national and international media is likely to have activated him to commence the process of retrieving the situation. On 17 May, after Gorbachev had left, Zhao tried to get a private meeting with Deng, but was instead summoned for a larger meeting at his residence that included the five members of the Politburo Standing Committee – Zhao Ziyang, Li Peng, Qiao Shi, Hu Qili and Yao Yilin – and a select group of the Elders. Blame for the catastrophe was squarely placed on Zhao. When Zhao weakly suggested that the editorial of 26 April was the real cause of the crisis, he was criticized. Deng made it clear that the line taken in that editorial was perfectly correct, and that the blame for the inability of the Party to quell the student protests could not be laid at anyone else's door than Zhao's since he was the general secretary. In *The Tiananmen Papers*, Deng is quoted as having said, 'Comrade Ziyang, that talk of yours on May 4 to the ADB was a turning point. Since then the student movement has steadily got worse.' Drawing a line in the sand, Deng informed the gathering that no further 'retreat' was possible, and he declared his decision to impose martial law in Beijing's urban districts. Zhao demurred. Deng would have none of it; he told Zhao that it was a matter of collective responsibility. 'The minority yields to the majority,' is what he reportedly exclaimed.[16] The Politburo Standing Committee then officially met and, if *The Tiananmen Papers* are to be believed, Zhao made one further attempt to question the decision on the declaration of martial law. Zhao returned to his residence and drafted a letter of resignation.[17] It was retrieved by Yang Shangkun before the letter could be distributed to the politburo, because Zhao was still trying every trick in the book to regain his power. Perhaps he felt that his threat of resignation might cause enough concern for a review. Having failed even in this effort, Zhao instead wrote privately to Deng Xiaoping the following day, 18 May, to reconsider the decision to impose martial law in Beijing, knowing full well that the decision had been a collective one and, thus, final.[18] Zhao, then, decided to proceed on leave on 19 May.

On 18 May, as the troops were being marshalled, Premier Li Peng made one final attempt to persuade the students to end the hunger strike, mainly for form's sake. It was broadcast on national television. He opened by saying that the meeting was 'only about one thing: how to get the fasting students out of their present plight'. An arrogant and combative Wu'er Kaixi, who came to the meeting in a striped hospital gown, retorted by saying 'as to how many questions we should discuss, it is for us to decide'.[19] Always with one eye on the dramatic element, he was not about to let the solemnity of this occasion stem his desire for publicity. Wang Dan and other student leaders reiterated their core demand – a retraction of the 26 April editorial which called the students' movement as 'turmoil'. Li Peng appeared to offer an olive branch when he told the student leaders that the Central Committee had never said that students were creating turmoil. But Li Peng had never been a subtle or nuanced person; rather, he appeared pugnacious and obstinate, and whatever chance there was of the dialogue achieving a desired outcome ended when he flatly refused to talk about the two demands made by the students, with an offhanded 'I will discuss it at an appropriate time'. It was a dialogue of the deaf. Li Peng never intended to compromise and the student leaders also appeared to be grandstanding. For both sides it was the final meeting.

At the crack of dawn on 19 May, Zhao Ziyang dramatically appeared in the square. The TV cameras were present to record the event. Megaphone in hand and with tear-filled eyes, Zhao made a last desperate attempt to hold on to power by going over the Central Committee directly to the masses. He asked the students to end the strike. Then, as if to show contrition and win sympathy, he uttered his famous last words in public: 'We came too late. We are sorry.' He added, 'If this situation continues, loses control, it will have serious consequences elsewhere.' In fact, it was already too late, and he knew these appeals were futile; his Party had already decided on military action. He had lost the power struggle; the consequences were to follow for the students and for him personally. Zhao Ziyang would disappear forever from public view.

Student protesters Chai Ling, with microphone, Wu'er Kaixi and Wang Dan address a crowd in Tiananmen Square on 27 May 1989.

Astrophysicist and dissenter Fang Lizhi at the University of Beijing in 1989.

The Goddess of Democracy, crafted out of Styrofoam by the student protesters, in Tiananmen Square on 1 June 1989.

Demonstrators at Tiananmen Square. The protests that were spearheaded by students soon found support from the liberal intelligentsia and went on for almost two months from 15 April to 3 June 1989.

Wu'er Kaixi (right), one of the prominent student leaders, walks past a police line on 19 May 1989.

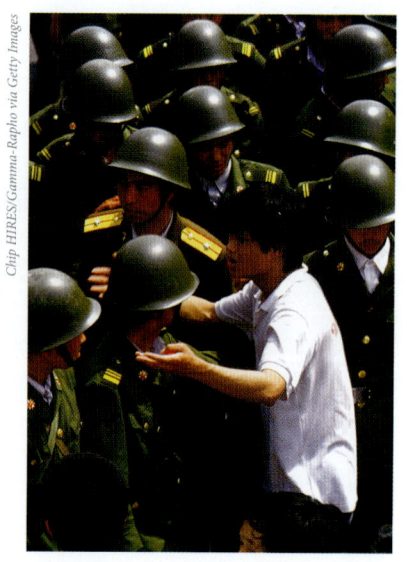

Confrontation between the protesters and the People's Liberation Army on 3 June 1989.

:CHAPTER 9:

Dousing the Flames

PREMIER LI PENG SPENT 19 MAY PREPARING FOR MARTIAL LAW. OVER 1,50,000 troops were moved to the vicinity of the capital. Zhao Ziyang had been relieved of his responsibilities and hence, Li Peng was the ranking member of the Politburo Standing Committee. At midnight he appeared on state television, flanked by Yao Yilin, Qiao Shi and Hu Qili. Zhao Ziyang's absence was glaring. In China appearance is everything. In the secretive system of the Communist Party of China, the order in which leaders enter or exit, their placement on the Tiananmen rostrum or at major events, and their absence, are intended to convey powerful political messages to the general public. Zhao Ziyang's absence informed the nation that he had exited the stage.

Li Peng delivered three messages in his long address, after first making it clear that he spoke for both Party and government high command. He opened by saying that the situation had been under control until the beginning of May, after which the turmoil revived again. Without naming Zhao, it was clear to the listening public that he was referring to his remarks at the ADB governors' meeting on 4 May as providing the spark for revival of the turmoil. Second, he explicitly referred to the unacceptable personal attacks on Deng Xiaoping. By invoking Deng's name, he cloaked his actions with the authority of the supreme leader. Lastly, he referred to a clique of unnamed people who wanted to achieve political objectives by fomenting chaos, and said, 'They have directed the spearhead against reform and opening up. If successful, it will turn China from a nation with a bright and hope-filled future into a China which is filled with despair and with no hope.' His intention, presumably, in referring to reform and opening up, was to reassure the public that there would be no sharp left turn again. Saying that 'resolute measures' needed to be taken, which was a euphemism for use of force, he asked the students to vacate the square and immediately cease all protest activity. It was an ultimatum. Li Peng became public enemy number one.

Sunday, 20 May. The mornings were still cool at that time of year, although by midday the onset of the summer becomes evident. Sunday mornings usually witness little activity on the roads. This Sunday was different. At 10 a.m. the State Council declared martial law in Beijing. The orders issued by the Beijing Municipal Government banned all demonstrations, strikes and social turmoil; prohibited attacks on government or PLA installations or personnel; and gave the People's Armed Police and the PLA the authority to 'use all means necessary' to quell the situation. Trucks carrying troops of the People's Liberation Army began to enter the city from different points and drive towards Tiananmen. This was the same force that had entered Beijing in 1949 as a liberating force. This time it came as a hostile force. Thousands of citizens descended on the roads to block the PLA from reaching the square. Traffic dividers were used as barriers. Citizens came out to block roads. The independent workers' union helped students with food and money. At a place called Gongzhufen, about seven kilometres from Tiananmen, over a hundred military trucks were blocked from entering the city.[1] An old woman remonstrated with the soldiers not to harm the students. Some presented flowers to the troops. Scenes like these were replicated across Beijing. People poured into the streets unmindful of their physical safety. Even at the height of the Cultural Revolution, the army had never faced such a predicament. On that day the citizens of Beijing brought the PLA to a virtual standstill.

Rumour was the flavour of the day. We saw helicopters making reconnaissance sorties down the Avenue of Eternal Peace. This was linked to reports that the 27th and 38th Armies of the PLA were poised to enter the city from the east and the west. A CNN report even went as far as to claim that some of the helicopters had showered flowers on the striking students in the square. Some claimed that sections of the PLA had revolted. We did not know what to believe at that point.

Since we had decided not to venture forth on the day that martial law was declared, our line of sight, so to speak, was the section from the China World Hotel to the Jianguomen flyover, where several of our diplomats had their homes. We saw many PLA trucks parked by the road side, filled with PLA troops, at a standstill and surrounded by citizens. The PLA troops were mostly very young rural men, who were confused by the resistance from the citizenry and their offers of food and drink. They became a public spectacle.

The Chinese state, which had been closely monitoring the foreign media and embassies that were regularly visiting the square, now decided to cut access to ground zero. Strict orders were issued prohibiting any foreigner from participating in or even reporting on anti-government activities. TV broadcasts became more difficult for the foreign media, though the Western print media still braved the martial law and continued to go to the square and talk to student leaders. From some of them, we gathered that on the ground the situation remained parlous and government orders were initially not implemented. Some of the Western journalists told us that there were open calls for resignations of Deng and Li Peng and appeals to the PLA not to follow orders. We saw one poster below the Jianguomen flyover that had a portrait of Deng Xiaoping along with an open letter from the people to Zhou Enlai, saying that Deng had betrayed the people fourteen years after Zhou's demise. There was another one purportedly from a PLA officer, assuring the citizens that the people's army would not harm them. There was no way of establishing the veracity of such material, but the fact that it was going up even after the declaration of martial law was an indication that the state had yet to establish its control.

By late evening the situation was turning surreal. Some of the PLA trucks had turned back. Rumours circulated that two companies of paratroopers would be dropped into the square after midnight, and we heard it from students who were cycling in various neighbourhoods to convey this information over a megaphone. Students were also gathering canisters of water in preparation for teargassing by the police in the square.

When 21 May dawned, there appeared to have been no moves made by the PLA overnight. Yet rumours circulated that they were at the railway and subway stations, fully prepared to emerge and strike. Some claimed to have heard movement of tanks outside the city at night. No newspapers were published, which was extraordinary, but all other public services continued as normal. Since the city appeared to be calm, we decided to venture out for a first-hand look. The numbers in the square rose through the day; by evening we estimated close to half a million in the general area. We saw students working at street corners, exhorting the citizenry to man the approaches to the city in order to block the security forces. Minivans and trucks filled with students shouting slogans against Li Peng and for democracy passed us. Wu'er Kaixi, dramatic to the end, was grandstanding at the crossing of the Avenue of Eternal Peace and Wangfujing Street, calling on people to fight to the bitter end. On reaching the square, we noticed several new posters that had a qualitatively different ring to them. They called on the National People's Congress deputies to overthrow the government. A person walked by carrying a portrait of Deng sporting a Hitler moustache and riding on a tank. Another poster lampooned Li Peng sitting on his Mercedes Benz while accepting money from the West Germans (Germany was still divided then) and the Japanese. One rumour that was interesting was that Li Peng had threatened the students with force; the two surviving marshals of the PLA – Nie Rongzhen and Xu Xianqian – had said that this was a fabrication. So charged was the atmosphere and so sparse was information about how the government intended to enforce martial law that the citizens kept vigil in the square and at key intersections for the second night running.

The Chinese media, in the initial days after the declaration of martial law, still remained 'independent'. On 21 May, for example, Xinhua News Agency staged a work slowdown and on 23 May they joined a demonstration. The *World Economic Herald*, which was now under supervision of the Shanghai municipal authorities, wrote on 24 May that press freedom 'is a duty of – not a favour granted to it by leaders – the media'.[2] Their courage in demonstrating independence in reporting even after the declaration of martial law, until it became impossible to do so, ought surely to redound to their credit. They could teach a thing or two to the Western media about courage under real pressure.

On 22 May, after two days and nights of rumour and frenzied rear guard action, we saw the first signs of normality return. Civilian police were manning the roads outside the diplomatic quarters, and later that same day they resumed duties along the entire Avenue of Eternal Peace. Roadblocks and crowds visibly declined in number. Helicopters dropped leaflets in the square that afternoon requesting the citizens to help the government restore order in the capital. It signalled that the leadership was acting to plan. But the square itself was far from being controlled by the authorities. A new poster, supposedly signed by seven former PLA generals, including Zhang Aiping and Yang Dezhi, calling on Beijing martial law headquarters not to open fire, was seen at the square.[3] Photocopies of the Hong Kong-based *Ming Bao* newspaper announcing the resignation of Hu Qili, Zhao's ally in the Politburo Standing Committee, were also pasted on the square. One eyewitness told us that nearly 300 Xinhua News Agency journalists had come to the square. As for foreign embassies, even the more laidback ones by now had their officers in the square, watching and reporting back to their capitals. Every rumour was magnified and reported. For instance, when the authorities announced that entry into the Forbidden City would be shut from 22 May, it was assumed that this was being done to allow the PLA to mass inside; nobody considered the fact that entry into the Forbidden City from Tiananmen Square had been rendered virtually impossible. Such innuendo and gossip, in hindsight, which was also being reported by foreign media and embassies, led to further misjudgement of the situation.

On 23 May, the foreign media reported a clash between the army and the students in the Fengtai area of the city, with casualties.

It seemed that the students had tried to block the troops from returning to their barracks. More surprising was a report carried by both the Xinhua and the *People's Daily*, quoting two unnamed PLA officers as saying that their orders were to patrol the streets and to assist the public. Clearly, the authorities were also worried about the citizens provoking young soldiers into retaliating, and were attempting to reassure the population that the army was not there to cause injury. A small sign that the government was beginning to get its act together.

Speculation about the leadership remained rife. Since 19 May, none of them had been seen in public or on television. Zhao's fate was not clear. There were rumours that he had resumed his position and that Li Peng had resigned. A Xinhua report of a meeting between the prime minister of Thailand and the Chinese ambassador, during which the former extended an invitation to Zhao Ziyang to visit Thailand, only fuelled reports about his return. Some Western diplomats claimed that in a briefing given to them by Foreign Minister Qian Qichen on 23 May, he made a reference to Zhao Ziyang; a Japanese diplomat also told us that his ambassador had been told by Vice Minister Tian Zengpei on the same day that Zhao was ill, but still the general secretary. These two instances were good examples of how a lack of understanding about Chinese politics could easily lead to incorrect deductions. The Chinese, unlike the West, will never outright admit to political changes. This is simply not their style. So long as Zhao had not publicly been removed, no Chinese official would have dared to say so, least of all to the 'foreign devils'. Hence, they would allude to illness or some other excuse to explain Zhao's public absence. The mistake that many made in those confusing times was to read the inputs from a Western perspective and, inevitably, arrive at an inaccurate conclusion. In fact, Deng had, reportedly, at a high-level Party meeting on 21 May, already said that Zhao Ziyang was fomenting division and splitting the Party, and would have to go, but the foreign media preferred to believe the gossip in the square. The problem was that those in the square knew exactly what the foreign correspondents wanted to hear, and gave it to them. One particularly telling example of this was when Australian diplomats claimed that the students had told them of having received assurances from PLA units in the capital, that these units would prevent fresh PLA units from assaulting the square, and that some of the units from the Beijing Military Region were in revolt. Such unsubstantiated rumour would no doubt have been reported to Western capitals, and probably gave rise to Western-sponsored reports about the likelihood of civil war inside China. The fact that *People's Daily* had reported that all seven military regions, including Beijing, had pledged loyalty to the Party was probably dismissed as propaganda.

If all did not appear to be well within the Chinese leadership, it was also true among the students. Fresh disagreements arose. The radicals were rapidly taking total control over the square. Those who felt that it might be prudent not to provoke the authorities under conditions of martial law were sidelined. Led by Chai Ling, the radicals had set up a Defend Tiananmen Headquarters in the square. Chai Ling became its self-proclaimed commander-in-chief. There were appeals to overthrow the regime. Student guard units were formed. There was endless infighting. Citizens tried to persuade the student leaders to open a dialogue with the government, but by then the radicals were in control and they claimed that nothing short of Li Peng's removal would satisfy them.

On 24 May, for the first time in many days, we drove around the square. There were still thousands there. Li Peng was the focal point of attack. Posters accusing him of creating bad blood between Deng and Zhao, and misleading Deng, were everywhere. But Deng was also being accused of manipulation from behind the scenes (*bei hou zhi hui*). The atmosphere inside the square had begun to take on a surreal form. Singers, including Taiwanese pop star Hou Dejian, and others performed for the students and onlookers. It was like a Chinese Woodstock at one level. But on the other hand, resources were running low. The square was squalid and smelly. The wailing sirens indicated that many strikers required medical attention. Moderate student leaders pressed for ending the hunger strike. They were promptly opposed by the radicals. It became a game of chicken amongst the student leadership, and the radicals taunted those who favoured a moderate line. Chai Ling claimed that there was even an attempt to kidnap her. In reality, the moderate approach had all but disappeared after 13 May.

The US embassy in Beijing was located at Xiushuijie in the old diplomatic district of Chao Yang in those days. Its diplomats had privileged access to Chinese officials, and many members of the diplomatic corps benefitted from the information they shared. However, as the crisis progressed and the leadership became embroiled in containing it, access became more difficult for US diplomats. They came to depend on their media, and on information from student leaders or intellectuals who were at odds with the regime. The problem was that they only got one side of the story. This was also the period of the Cold War, and Western diplomats were as ideologically motivated as their Eastern bloc colleagues. They often tended to read more into a situation than was warranted by the facts on the ground. This is what happened as the crisis threatened to take a violent turn after the declaration of martial law.

Declassified US documents exposed the extent of the misjudgement. For example, on 21 May, the newly arrived US ambassador James Lilley, a CIA veteran, sent this assessment to the State Department: 'This current PRC government is not a strong one; it may not last long; despite its ability to suppress an uprising. What is happening here in opposition to the authorities has a permanence about it. It is not going away.'[4] To be fair to the ambassador, he did qualify his assessment by adding that this was preliminary, but to the State Department thousands of miles away, also preoccupied with other global issues, any reporting which appeared to have the ring of truth quickly became fact. Thus, for instance, the secretary of state's morning briefing for 2 June claimed, 'Two weeks after declaring martial law in Beijing, hardliners remain unable to resolve the leadership crisis or to remove students from Tiananmen Square.'[5]

We now know Deng had already resolved the leadership crisis by then, and was only days away from taking military action to end the stand-off. He had seen many such situations in his long political career. He had prevailed against the odds on more than one occasion. He had seen death from close quarters in war and while in power. Had the Gang of Four prevailed in 1976, Deng, in all probability, would not have been left alive. For Deng, the Party was everything, and he was determined to see China re-emerge as a global power. As his biographer Ezra Vogel said, despite the subsequent criticism that he would receive, Deng never once doubted that he had made the right decision. He stuck with it.

His first priority was to unite a divided Party. He began by summoning an enlarged meeting of the politburo on 20 May, at which all the Elders were present, and he outlined the scale of the problem. He wanted their support on his actions. On 25 May, his co-equal, Chen Yun, who still headed the Central Advisory Committee (CAC), said that the CAC supported the 'Party Centre'. Affirmations of support quickly followed from other Elders – Peng Zhen, Wang Zhen and Li Xiannian. Simultaneously, he had to tackle Zhao's efforts to involve the National People's Congress, the 'rubber-stamp' Parliament of China, in the matter. Zhao had written to its chairman, Wan Li, to return early from the United States where he was on an official visit, and to convene a meeting to hear reports on the student protests. Wan Li had initially obliged, but when he landed in Shanghai, he was 'persuaded' to rescind the decision.

Once Deng had united the leadership behind his actions, his next priority was to cut the lines of communication between students in various cities of China. After 4 May, many students had come in from other cities. They would then return from Tiananmen Square to their native places carrying impressions and images of student protests, which in turn would generate more student activities in other cities. In the early months of the Cultural Revolution, when Mao Zedong had wanted to rebuild his image among the youth, he had encouraged university and high-school students to travel all over China for free on trains. The system was called '*zhuan lian*'. It had led to immeasurable chaos on the public transportation system and damage to public property. Many of these students joined the Red Guards. Premier Zhou Enlai finally put a stop to it with the help of the Chinese army after these young hoodlums began to destroy China's cultural heritage and environment. Deng had witnessed at first-hand what chaos students on the move could unleash, and focussed on curbing it. On 25 May, a directive was issued by the State Council to the railway authorities to stop all students from boarding trains for

Beijing. In an effort to break physical connectivity between the capital and the regions, railway officials were to be held personally responsible for enforcing this directive.

On the same day, the leadership also began to bring the media under its control. Propaganda has always been an indispensable tool in the communist toolbox, and Deng began the process of retrieving the space that the Chinese media had gained after 9 May, when Hu Qili had loosened controls. With Hu Qili also having been removed from power along with Zhao, PLA units began to systematically occupy the headquarters of major TV channels and newspapers in Beijing and other cities in order to bring reporting back under the Party's control. Sporadic defiance would continue until 4 June, but gradually radio and TV as well as the *People's Daily* started referring to the Party line that 'stability' was the order of the day. By the end of May, pro-government reporting had resumed.

Once the government had got a grip on the levers of power including the propaganda machinery, Deng turned his attention to the students. The original hunger strikers had withdrawn. The Beijing Students' Autonomous Federation had expelled Wu'er Kaixi. A new Hunger Strike Headquarters came into being with Chai Ling in the lead, supported by her spouse Feng Congde and Zhang Boli. They decided to 'defend' the square. Chai Ling made those present in the square take a solemn oath: 'I swear I will protect the republic and Tiananmen Square with my young life. Heads can roll, blood can flow, but the People's Square can never be lost. We are willing to fight to the last person.' At one point, she called for the overthrow of the 'illegal government headed by Li Peng'.[6] The situation inside the square now turned desperate because the overcrowding, lack of funds and absence of any organized advice resulted in individual 'warlords' running their own little domains. Chai Ling, who, like Wu'er Kaixi, was overly dramatic and prone to mood swings, suddenly decided to leave amid constant infighting among the student leadership at the Hunger Strike Headquarters, and just as suddenly returned the next day, 29 May, saying that though she wanted to quit people had told her that this was not the right moment to do that.[7]

In the absence of credible sources of information, the foreign press began to peddle rumour. One that gained particular currency was the impending return of Zhao Ziyang. Students in the square were mixing fact and rumour to sensationalize matters and the foreign press, hungry for news, did not wait to verify it. One study which analysed the role of the Beijing-based US media in this crisis has opined that, in retrospect, media built up public expectations that the movement would succeed.[8] Perhaps the expectations of violence immediately after the declaration of martial law, which did not materialize, might have led media to hope for the 'best'. There is no gainsaying the fact that foreign media substantially reinforced the views in many embassies in Beijing that the PLA had 'revolted' against the Party and refused to act on orders, that the 'liberals' were pushing for Zhao's return and that use of force may not be possible. After 26 May, when the Party had regained control over the Chinese media, the foreign media tended to ignore the reports they were putting out, and thus what was being read outside China was entirely one-sided and often based on a mixture of fact and fiction.

From the Indian embassy's perspective, the assessment was different. From 25 May, we noted small signs that the leadership was gaining the upper hand. The central radio broadcasts referred to Deng as 'Chairman' Deng. The *People's Daily* also published a letter from the top PLA levels to the troops commending them on their loyalty and discipline, in which there were references to Deng, Yang Shangkun and Li Peng by their official titles. Zhao's disappearance from public view was also a pointer. We had also heard unconfirmed reports that Yang Shangkun had addressed the Central Military Commission on 24 May and made references to the involvement of individual leaders in complicating the political situation. Therefore, we reported to the Ministry of External Affairs in New Delhi that Deng appeared to have prevailed in the political struggle within the Party. Within the embassy, we debated on whether the delay in announcing Zhao's dismissal was because the purge was targeting other top-ranking leaders as well, or because the leadership was simply unable to decide on a successor. For us in the embassy, the big question was whether Deng had been weakened by the episode to the point where his rivals could install their own successor.

From 27 May onwards, there were even more indications that the leadership had united and reasserted control. Li Peng met foreign ambassadors. Chinese media reported that all Chinese provincial party committees had formally supported the Party. Central organs like the Central Party School and Ministry of Foreign Affairs also lined up behind the government. Elements from both these organizations had been seen in the square in support of students, and therefore one could presume that dissent had been crushed there. More and more leaders, including the chairman of the National Peoples Commission, Wan Li, referred to a 'plot' to create unrest by a handful of forces with help from outside and supported the declaration of martial law. Since none except Li Peng had appeared in public after 19 May, those who wanted to clutch at straws continued to do that.

It is curious why the leaders did not yet attempt to 'pacify' the square and it is possible that they still had hopes of resolving it peacefully. The situation took another, final, turn inside the square. The statue of a woman made of Styrofoam and plaster was assembled section by section. They called it the Goddess of Democracy, somewhat naively as they didn't have any real understanding of democracy and the freedoms it brought. It was modelled on the Statue of Liberty, though the goddess held the flaming torch in both hands. Those who created or installed it had little practical knowledge or understanding of democracy. The student politics in the square resembled the Communist Party of China to a greater degree than it did any kind of democratic organization. There was hardly any tolerance for alternative points of view. Gangs were operating as the sword arm of different factions, and the leadership engaged in turf wars and power play at the cost of the larger movement. The Goddess of Democracy was formally unveiled on 30 May, which was the tenth day of martial law in Beijing. It faced Mao's giant portrait on the Tiananmen in a gesture of defiance. Thousands came to the square to witness this event, but it was the last gasp of a dying movement – a novelty rather than an inspiration to gear up for the final confrontation with the state.

From subsequent accounts and information, we now know that the government was already in the midst of advanced preparation to act. The Elders had met twice between 21 and 26 May. They settled on Shanghai's party secretary, Jiang Zemin, as the next general secretary to succeed Zhao Ziyang. In doing so, they were reaching beyond three eligible sitting members of the Politburo Standing Committee – Premier Li Peng, Vice Premier Yao Yilin and Qiao Shi who was the security supremo. On the surface it seemed a strange choice, but it was classic Deng. For him, there could be no deviation from his dream of 'reform and opening up'. For that reason, both Li Peng and Yao Yilin were unacceptable. Although Li Peng had loyally carried out Deng's orders of imposing the martial law, Deng had no illusions about Li Peng where economic policy was concerned. Why Qiao Shi was overlooked is not clear, but perhaps the Elders did not want the security tsar to head the Party. Jiang Zemin was a safe bet. He had proved his loyalty early on during the crisis over the handling of the *World Economic Herald* and Qin Benli, and he had been able to deal with the student protests in Shanghai without much disruption of economic life or use of extreme measures. He did not have strong ties with any faction since he was merely one of the politburo members, and he had no charisma. The choice suited Deng and he allowed the Elders to believe that it was their choice. Thus Jiang Zemin became the core of the so-called third generation of Chinese leadership.[9] Li Peng must have been deeply disappointed.

Before taking any decisive action in the square, Deng needed to complete one final task. He had to ensure the loyalty of the PLA. He had been apprised of the fraternization between the troops and the citizenry in many parts of the city since 20 May. Mostly callow and uneducated, the young men had been subjected to entreaties by citizens and admonition by women old enough to be their grandmothers. They had been fed, sung to and occasionally roughed up. Their trucks were surrounded and blockaded. Deng used the services of Yang Shangkun, president of China and sometime general in the PLA, and his brother Yang Baibing, who was the army's chief political commissar, for this purpose. He also roped in two of China's marshals – Nie Rongzhen and Xu Xianqian. By 31 May, the army had fully aligned itself with the Party. All the elements in Deng's strategy for taking decisive action to end the 'counterrevolutionary turmoil' were now in place.

Western diplomats were claiming otherwise. A number of them told us that units of armies from the Jinan, Chengdu and Guangdong Military Regions had surrounded the capital. The British were particularly egregious in their propaganda, and because the rest of the West thought they understood China better than the others, their word was usually taken at face value. One British diplomat told us that the tear gas cannisters that people had reportedly seen being deployed were in fact surface-to-air missiles. Why they ignored the public appearances of the two deputy secretaries general of the PLA, Admiral Liu Huaqing and General Hong Xuezhi, who inspected the troops on martial law duties on 30 May, or a public appearance by General Chi Haotian, the chief of PLA general staff, the following day remains a mystery. It was a clear signal that the military was preparing to act. Perhaps the West trusted too much in the opponents of the regime.

In a complete display of unity, the Party Centre and the State Council issued a joint communique on 31 May. Its objective was to signal to the general population that there were no longer differences within the leadership, and as a warning to the citizenry that the authorities were ready to act. The communique attributed the turmoil to a 'very small clique' who wanted to create chaos, and was careful not to make any reference to the student protests. A final warning was, however, delivered to students to return to their classes on campuses, to the citizens of Beijing to permit the restoration of normality in city services, and to the media to fall in line by starting a propaganda campaign to expose the 'conspiracy and activities of the small clique'. Party and government functionaries who continued to violate discipline or orders were also put on notice. The local population understood that Deng was ready to act. Students ended their hunger strike and a trickle of students began to leave the square on 1 and 2 June, leaving only a small rump along with hundreds of tents, banners and piles of rubbish.

Deng first sent in regular troops on 3 June. Many were not in combat gear. From our balcony we saw troops dressed in white singlets and regulation trousers, and carrying backpacks, pass in front of our building along the Avenue of Eternal Peace. They occupied the main bridges and intersections along the second ring road which roughly corresponded with the gates of the Old City, effectively putting a chokehold over all access points to the square. Citizens continued to throw up barricades to impede the movement of trucks and armoured personnel carriers in the city. We saw some people deflating the tyres of the parked PLA vehicles near the Jianguomen flyover. We heard that the nearest the troops got to the square was the old Beijing Hotel.

In the evening fresh troops were inducted. The new troops were helmeted and armed with automatic weapons. The US embassy sent a cable to the State Department on 3 June stating that the 'force option is real'.[10] At 7 p.m., China Central Television made an emergency announcement of the martial law enforcement troops, saying all necessary measures will be taken to restore law and order. Resistance continued. We witnessed a small group of troops dismounted and tried to jog down the Avenue of Eternal Peace, after their vehicle's tyres were deflated, but we could see the citizenry forcing them to turn back near the Friendship Store. But the announcements over the radio and television made it clear that this time there might be no turning away. The population was being warned to stay indoors.

I recall being woken by noise of armour moving down the Avenue of Eternal Peace. It was 5 a.m. on 4 June. I counted at least fifteen tanks, several armoured personnel carriers (APCs) and troop trucks sweeping down the avenue. The man-made barriers were no match for battle tanks; they were simply crushed or pushed aside. Citizens ran for cover. Helicopters hovered above the moving columns. There were reports of automatic weapon fire in other parts of the city, but none could be heard from where we were.

Foreign media were claiming that the army had fired into crowds with several hundred casualties. We witnessed an ambulance and an army truck being set afire just outside the Friendship Store, but soldiers were not attacked. Resistance was largely passive, though there were reports, and later images, of petrol bombs being thrown at the APCs.

There is no accurate account of what happened in Tiananmen Square on the night of 3–4 June. Movement of foreign media had been severely restricted, and in any case, by that time, they were groping for information because their sources were drying up as Deng regained control over the state apparatus. The best that can be surmised is that fully armed troops forced their way past barricades and crowds. In the process, it cannot be ruled out that some firing took place in areas where the citizenry attempted to block troop movement by force. There are reports of rocks and Molotov cocktails being thrown. The troops responded with live ammunition.[11] There are credible eyewitness accounts of people dying of gunshot wounds, but these casualties were mostly bystanders and people blocking the advance of the troops.

The PLA surrounded the square after midnight of 3–4 June and demanded that the remaining students vacate it. Chai Ling says she asked those who wished to go to leave immediately. There were differences among the student leaders as to whether or not they should talk to the troop commander, and it seems that finally the Taiwanese singer Hou Dejian and intellectual activist Liu Xiaobo both went. The troop commander advised them to tell the students to leave the square. While this was being debated, armed troops from inside the Great Hall of the People descended on Tiananmen Square. With no choice left, the remaining students left at dawn on 4 June. The Communist Party of China regained its control over Tiananmen Square, likely without firing a shot inside the square.

According to those who were present, and who spoke much later to the Western press, there was certainly no killing inside the square.[12] By mid-morning the next day, troops were fully in control of the square and its vicinity. Mopping-up operations were under way in other parts. This continued through 5 June, and at least twice a motorized tank column rolled up and down the Avenue of Eternal Peace in front of our apartment block in a show of strength. Feeble attempts by some citizens to erect barriers were quickly abandoned. Tanks were parked at key intersections. This time the citizenry made no attempt to approach them.

One eyewitness, a diplomat from Chile,[13] who later briefed the US embassy, had driven to the square around 2100 hours on 3 June to fetch his ambassador who was dining at the Movenpick Hotel on the western side of Tiananmen. He said that troops had filled the approach roads to the square but had not impeded his passage. He had parked just east of the Museum of Chinese History, and walked into the square. He had heard sporadic gunfire but no automatic fire. He told the US embassy that troops were mostly armed with anti-riot gear. He also claimed that most tents in the square were empty when the tanks rolled over them. There were no signs of a massacre. In the early hours, the remaining students, arms linked together, left the square through the south-east corner, after which troops cleared the square of the tents and garbage. His account matched the narrative that the student leaders would offer many years later.

Violence did occur in other parts of the city. Troops fired upon citizens or students who resisted martial law,[14] but there were also instances of the troops themselves being assaulted and killed. Some of our embassy personnel who had gone to Xiyuan Hotel that evening to enquire about the welfare of Indian nationals reported seeing fifteen burnt-out vehicles. The exact number of casualties is not likely to be known unless the communist authorities disclose the truth. Lacking credible inputs, the US embassy and foreign media began to give wildly speculative accounts of the happenings on the night of 3–4 June. Declassified US government documents show that the estimates of casualty figures increased from 180 to 300 in the briefing paper for the secretary of state on 4 June, to 500 to 2,600 a couple of days later, and the number of those injured was put at 10,000. The 5 June briefing paper claimed that 'hundreds' of military vehicles 'including at least thirty-four tanks and numerous APCs' had been destroyed, and some students, having seized APCs and weapons, were 'vowing to resist'.[15]

The US embassy continued to treat rumour and speculation as fact and report it to Washington. An embassy cable reported that the PLA opened machine gun fire in the square, which was subsequently found to be untrue. Another cable claimed that, according to one report, Deng Xiaoping was giving attack orders from a hospital bed.[16] This too turned out to be false when Deng made an appearance a few days later in public. Yet another cable on 6 June suggested imminent hostilities between the 27th Army deployed at the Jianguomen flyover and other unnamed PLA units, and rumours of infighting in the PLA.[17] The US ambassador even alluded to this in a Voice of America broadcast. It is not always possible to get accurate information in a crisis, but US diplomats abandoned even the normal caution that should have been adopted when reporting back to headquarters. Many diplomats, who were living in the diplomatic compound overlooking the Jianguomen bridge and thus had a bird's-eye view of the area, knew that the rumours were untrue. Presumably, US diplomats, who were staying in the same compound, also had these facts, and yet a US embassy cable on 7 June claimed that there was fighting between PLA units, and artillery fire had been heard in south-west Beijing on the night of 6 June. Recently released British archives tell a similar story. The British ambassador, Sir Alan Donald, reportedly sent a telegram to the Foreign and Commonwealth Office, claiming that 10,000 fatalities were a minimum estimate, and providing a dramatic description of how tanks mowed down students in the square and then ran over their bodies time and again.[18] He claimed that this information had been provided by sources (unnamed) in the government, but eyewitness accounts by student leaders themselves decisively refute such an account. In the fog of war or revolution it is not always easy to get facts, but responsible governments are expected to desist from reporting rumour as fact. This is especially the case when they are representatives of nations that wield extraordinary influence in the shaping of global public opinion, as in the case of both the United States and the United Kingdom. And yet, the news that went out to the world through the Western media and from Western representatives in China were mostly half-truths mixed with downright fiction. It was not a proud moment for the Free World or its Free Press.

Law and order began to return to Beijing. After the initial days of resistance, the barriers that had blocked the main roads were cleared. APCs and PLA troops were stationed at all major intersections to deter miscreants or further protests. The stern warnings left nobody in any doubt that the regime would use force again if needed. After 6 June the city witnessed no further activity by citizens. One curious incident happened though. PLA soldiers suddenly opened fire on the diplomatic compound at Jianguomen Wai with live ammunition at 10 a.m. on 7 June.[19] The bullets shattered windows and entered several apartments facing the Avenue of Eternal Peace. It was claimed by the authorities that they suspected a rooftop sniper. It was a crude warning to the diplomatic corps that the Chinese state was done with their shenanigans. Much later, Ambassador James Lilley claimed that Larry Wortzel, an officer with the defence attaché's office, was given advance warning by a Chinese contact that the PLA would fire on the diplomatic compound.[20] If this is correct, the US embassy did not share this information with other diplomatic missions, at least not with the Indian embassy. The incident spooked the entire diplomatic community. Within days, most Western embassies had emptied their diplomatic staff from Beijing. In hindsight, the complicity of some Chinese authorities in this incident cannot be ruled out. The Chinese are very good at messaging. If they had any part in this, they too acted without judgement.

In the Indian embassy the ambassador convened a meeting to discuss the shooting incident. One of our officers, Political Attaché Sikri's residence, had also been hit by bullets but the occupants of the apartment escaped unhurt. We took into account the visual scenes that many of us had witnessed in the past week. The ambassador was responsible for the safety of embassy personnel and staff, of course, but there were also other considerations in play. India–China relations had normalized after Prime Minister Rajiv Gandhi's visit to China in December 1988. We had turned the page on one of the most painful chapters in our history – the military debacle of 1962. We could look ahead to better times. Any action we took which might look like we were joining the West in indicting the regime in China could complicate the restoration of normality. It was a long and hard discussion. Finally, we took the collective view that while it was our duty as officers of the government to remain in our posts, we could not risk the safety of families. It was decided that they would return to India on the next direct British Airways flight from Beijing to New Delhi. Delhi was not pleased with this decision and made that amply clear to the ambassador. If the Chinese were unhappy, it was never expressed to us nor shown in any manner in the ensuing months.

Deng Xiaoping felt confident enough about the situation to make a public appearance on 9 June. Virtually, the entire leadership – anybody who was fit enough to walk and stand – lined up behind him in a clear message to the public that the Communist Party of China was united. His opening words to the martial law troops were, 'The storm was bound to come. It was fortunate to have a large group of veteran comrades at this time,' thus underscoring collective responsibility for the action that he took. He reaffirmed that the description of the protests as 'turmoil' in the *People's Daily* editorial of 26 April was correct. He dismissed the allegation that concerns over corruption had led to the protests, labelling it an 'excuse' for those who wanted to overthrow the Party and establish a bourgeois republic that would be entirely dependent on the West. While commending the PLA for carrying out its task, he also admonished them by saying, 'In future we must never again let people take away our weapons.' He had two clear messages for the West. First, he warned the Americans about their actions in sanctioning China over the suppression of the student protests, adding, 'From now on, as soon as a trend emerges, we should not allow it to spread.' Thus, he made it clear that China would place its own security above US concerns. Secondly, he unambiguously reiterated that China was committed to a market economy with the words: 'There cannot be any change in this policy. We should never change China into a closed country.' US commercial interests would not be hurt and it would be business as usual.

The media, completely back under state control by then, put out the first authoritative version of events that would mark the beginning of the cover-up. It alleged that despite declaration of martial law, a 'small minority' tried to topple the government in an attempt to capture power with tactics like 'storm the Bastille', and to place state leaders under arrest. It clearly referred to the foreign hand. Authorities claimed that the army was compelled to act after a police station was attacked on 1 June, and martial law troops were disarmed and beaten on 3 June. Threat to life was cited as reason for military action. It went on to give graphic descriptions of how vehicles were burnt and PLA soldiers were killed in Liu Bu Kou, Guangqumen, Chongwenmen and other parts of the city, and more than 450 vehicles were destroyed. In the final part of its account, the state averred that students left the square voluntarily, and that the entire account of 'bloodletting' was a complete untruth. The full account should be read to understand how the Communist Party of China has crafted its narrative to suggest that it was a handful who tried to destroy the people's state. It has remained the defining narrative till date, and most Chinese know nothing else about it.

Having put out its own authoritative version, the arrests started almost immediately. Official media asked people to report on those who had engaged in the destruction of public property. A notice went out to citizens that those who protected or hid 'counterrevolutionary elements' would be severely dealt with, which meant that anybody who had knowledge of such people should come forward or face reprisal. In one case, they even broadcast a clip of unknown people setting alight a military vehicle and inviting citizens to report if they recognized any of them. The so-called illegal unions of students and workers were outlawed under Martial Law Order No. 10, and their leaders were detained. On 9 June, China Central Television broadcast a list of the twenty-one most wanted, for their participation in stirring up 'turmoil' in the country. Wang Dan's name was first on the list, Wu'er Kaixi was the second, and Chai Ling was fourth while her spouse and fellow radical at the Defend Tiananmen Headquarters, Feng Congde, was thirteenth. Only seven of the twenty-one most wanted students escaped. Wang Dan was arrested; Wu'er Kaixi and Chai Ling escaped to Hong Kong. Activists like Wang Juntao, Chen Ziming, Dai Qing and Liu Xiaobo were also arrested and tried. Although an arrest warrant was issued for Fang Lizhi, and his spouse, the US embassy got to him first. On the night of 5 June, Political Counsellor Raymond Burghardt escorted the couple to the US ambassador's residence on Guang Hua Road.[21] First Secretary Bill Stanton was appointed as minder. He was to be their guest for a further 385 days.

All that remained was to tie up the final threads in this long tale. Zhao had already been purged from all his positions in the Party and state, but as was the case with his predecessor, Hu Yaobang, the formalities remained to be completed. Zhao was invited to attend a meeting of the politburo on 19 June to make a full confession, known in communist Chinese parlance as 'self-criticism'. He tried to take the legal road, speaking about the illegality of decisions taken by the Politburo Standing Committee in his absence, since he was still the general secretary. He also tried to explain his comments to Gorbachev when they met in May. But if it was for Deng's benefit, it was to no avail because Deng had stayed away. Then, he was formally voted out from office. The decision was formalized at the fourth plenary meeting of the Central Committee on 23–24 June, which also delivered the final word on the events in Tiananmen Square. This version declared that a 'very small number of people' caused counterrevolutionary turmoil with the motive of overthrowing the leadership of the Party and the People's Republic; the actions taken by Central Committee were both 'necessary' and 'correct'; the older generation of leaders represented by Deng Xiaoping had acted with wisdom; Zhao Ziyang had made mistakes in supporting the turmoil and in splitting the Party at a time of 'life-and-death struggle', for which he bore unshakeable responsibility. Zhao was dismissed from all offices and investigation into the case was to continue. This was the last the Party spoke of the Tiananmen Square incident, and their decision was cast in stone. To this day no leader of China has chosen to reverse the verdict delivered on 24 June 1989, and a blanket of silence has descended over this matter. Thirty years on, for the majority of young Chinese, the Tiananmen Square incident is an aberration, a distant fact that they know nothing about beyond the Party line.

The Chinese had one last loose end to tie up. They needed to ensure that relations with the United States, from which they had benefitted a great deal, were not damaged irreparably. The US had imposed sanctions – no military sales, suspension of military exchanges and no World Bank loans. Fang Lizhi had not yet become a cause célèbre, but both sides knew where he was and the Chinese saw this as proof of the US hand in the unrest. The Chinese need not have worried. The US abandoned its policy almost immediately, by sending National Security Advisor Scowcroft and Deputy Secretary of State Eagleburger to Beijing on 1 July, less than three weeks after the alleged blood had been spilled in the square. A declassified memorandum from the State Department, of 29 June 1989, said that President Bush intended to 'do all he can to maintain a steady course because he believes deeply that a solid relationship between the People's Republic of China and the United States is in the interests of world peace and international stability'. He ordered Scowcroft and Eagleburger to travel to China to 'reach an understanding on each side of the concerns and intentions of the other'. If this was realpolitik, it was also a searing lesson in how great democracies abandon publicly avowed principles, such as human rights, in self-interest without having the courage to say so openly, because they fear their own public opinion will see how hollow they are. Within a year, Sino-American relations were back to business as usual, and the US turned its attention to the ending of the Cold War and the establishment of the United States as the world's indispensable power. Reassured that China would remain open, it was Wall Street not the White House that would determine China policy. The consequences of that mercantilist approach are only just beginning to be recognized today.

:CHAPTER 10:

Doubling Down

THE TIANANMEN SQUARE INCIDENT OF 4 JUNE 1989 MARKED THE END of a decade of political and economic experimentation by the communists. In 1979, with China reeling from the disaster of the Great Proletarian Cultural Revolution, and facing an uncertain political future, revival seemed difficult. Yet the Chinese Communist Party had proved capable of reinventing itself in 1949 when a rebel army transformed itself into a government, and it would prove so again under Deng's able leadership. The economic reforms that took place between 1980 and 1988 laid down the foundations for the transformation of the Chinese economy into what is likely to become the world's largest economy by 2030. Politically, too, Deng was able to introduce systemic reform that stabilized the leadership and minimized the risk of China reverting to a neo-Maoist state, even though the fall of Zhao Ziyang in May 1989 was Deng's second failed attempt at ensuring an orderly succession. At the meeting on 21 May 1989, after the imposition of martial law in Beijing, Deng had reportedly admitted that the problem lay within the Party.[1] Deng and the Elders worked out a new modus vivendi, beginning with a consensus between Deng and Chen Yun on the two basic propositions for the Party's future. First, economic reform and opening up must proceed unhindered and without reversal, and the one essential criterion for carrying the economic reform agenda forward was firm opposition to Western political thought or ideas and the preservation of the absolute rule of the Communist Party of China.[2]

Second, political reform was not open for discussion. The highest principle of politics would be the perpetuation of the Party's control on power. A new political arrangement was intended to give effect to this principle.

What about the 'democratic' upsurge that had manifested itself on the streets of Beijing and other Chinese cities for more than fifty days? While the rest of the world speculated whether the 1989 incident was the first flush of democracy in China, Deng understood his people. He felt that most of the Chinese people valued stability and order, had a deep-seated fear of turmoil, and desired a better life. On this basis, Deng built a new Party line that became the bedrock of China's politics for the next three decades. He decreed that domestic political and social stability was the indispensable condition for the country's continued development, and that only the Chinese Communist Party could ensure that the two went hand in hand. Deng believed that a clear iteration of the new paradigm would reassure the Chinese people that the Party intended to press on with economic development and would not return to the days of political struggle, mass agitation or Cultural Revolution anarchy. He was conscious of Western condemnation and disapproval but is believed to have remarked that there was no need for China to check out the look on a foreigner's face before it decided what to do.[3] Deng rightly guessed that the world's principal concern in 1989 was not with human rights but the possibility that China might go into isolation again. He urged the new leadership to project a clear commitment to reform and stay the course on policies like joint ventures with foreign capital and the special economic zones. The West had just begun to make serious investments in China, often on preferential terms that guaranteed handsome returns on capital. Given the choice between benefitting from the Chinese economy and sacrificing it for the sake of human rights, the West chose profit over principles. Deng was proved correct in his assumption.

Deng Xiaoping also paid close attention to the mechanics of the new political arrangement. To stabilize the collective leadership he came up with the idea of a leadership core. Declaring Mao Zedong to be the core of the first-generation leadership, and himself as the core of the second generation, he proposed the idea of collective responsibility along with division of powers,[4] with the general secretary of the Communist Party of China as the anchor (core). Under Deng's new system, all the top leaders, that is, the members of the Politburo Standing Committee, would exercise their individual responsibilities and power within the collective leadership, and the core would provide the unifying principle. Jiang Zemin was selected as the core of the third-generation leadership. Deng probably thought this might be the only way to avoid the re-emergence of factional rivalries that might threaten the Party's unity again. With this new arrangement in place, the brief period of openness in China came to an end and the veil of secrecy covered the inner workings of the Communist Party once more. Leaders after Deng rarely offered the outside world a glimpse of internal debates and differences in the same way as in 1989 again.

The fall of the Berlin Wall later that year, and the collapse of the Soviet Union and its satellite states in the ensuing three years, deeply shocked the Chinese leadership and taught them another important lesson. After a thorough study of the causes for the downfall of the Soviet Union, the Chinese communists concluded that it had disintegrated because of ideological confusion, and the subsequent loss of political control had allowed external forces (particularly the Americans) to bring about its collapse. The Chinese leadership drew the inference that America, and the West, in general, desired to effect regime change in communist states. Western support for and propaganda in favour of pro-democracy forces during the Tiananmen crisis were seen as attempts to undermine the Party and to weaken its grip on power. Following the disintegration of the Soviet Union, the Chinese leadership presumed that China was now the main political target of the United States, and seemed to regard America as the primary existential threat to the survival and perpetuation of the Communist Party of China. Henceforth, within the Party's deepest recesses, America was apparently public enemy number one. Yet China also required American capital, technology and know-how for its economic development. It was this delicate balancing act between China's economic needs and the requirements of national security that brought forth Deng Xiaoping's strategy known as *'taoguang yanghui, yousuo zuowei'* (biding time by keeping a low profile). Deng decided that until China grew economically and militarily strong, it would not give the West any cause for offence or complaint as long as they participated in and helped its economic growth. China focussed on providing the West with the economic opportunities to profit from its development, while benefitting from the influx of foreign capital and technology. In the international arena China kept a low profile, appearing to cooperate with the American-led liberal global order.

Deng Xiaoping's post-1989 arrangements allowed for the remarkable transformation of China over the next two decades (1991–2010). Economic reforms were implemented in five areas – fiscal, or the principle of matching revenue and expenditure; financial, including development of capital, monetary, foreign exchange and gold markets; management of floating exchange rate; private investment; and the construction of a legal system for business. Availability of surplus farm labour for employment in the burgeoning manufacturing sector and large-scale capital investment in infrastructure, financed from domestic savings that improved the logistics and transportation network, along with tax policies that benefitted foreign investors after 1990, led to a surge in foreign direct investment (FDI). In 1991 China secured just US $4.37 billion in FDI, by 2005 it had grown to US $30 billion, and it peaked at US $196 billion in 2016. There were reportedly 445,244 foreign invested enterprises (FIEs) employing 55.2 million people in 2010. In addition, these FIEs were responsible for a significant level of China's foreign trade. At their peak, FIEs accounted for 58.3 per cent of exports in 2005 and 59.7 per cent of imports.[5] China doubled its GDP every eight years after 1979. From 1991 to 2015, China's real annual GDP growth was above 7 per cent. This was reflected in the statistics for China's global merchandise trade. It grew from a mere US $117 billion in 1990 to a staggering US $3 trillion by 2010. China's skilful diplomacy in persuading the West to sponsor its entry into the World Trade Organization in 2001 played no small part in integrating China into the global division of labour. By 2010, China had literally become the world's factory. Not for nothing did the World Bank call it the fastest sustained expansion by a major economy in history.

What the world at large did not comprehend at the time was that these developments perfectly served the Communist Party of China's key objective of maintaining political and social stability, and the preservation of the Party's absolute power. The Western world hoped that its economic and financial assistance to China would, over time, make the Chinese more like 'us'. In fact, the Chinese simply bided their time, as Deng had foretold, and continued to benefit from easy access to Western capital and technology for a generation until China became a true competitor to the West. It was only towards the end of the first decade of this century that the Americans realized that China was not going to be the responsible stakeholder in the way that the US had imagined. By the time this realization dawned, the economies of China and the West were closely intertwined and China's economy was integral to the world's economic recovery after the global financial crisis. Today claims are made that China has used unfair trade practices such as undervalued currency and subsidies to flood the Western markets with low-cost goods, or to promote domestic firms by denying market access to foreign companies, and there are reports of widespread infringement and theft of intellectual property. But during the heydays of Western and American companies in China (1990–2010) this was an acceptable risk for partaking of the huge benefits the Chinese market and its labour force offered. If China has today become the world's largest economy in terms of purchasing power parity, the largest-trading nation, a significant exporter of capital and the largest holder of foreign reserves, it is both because of the hard work of the Chinese people and due to the short-sighted strategies of Western businesses and governments.

On the political side, since stability was now the overriding objective of all policy, Deng's successors did nothing dramatic or extreme, and governance under presidents Jiang Zemin and Hu Jintao (1989–2013) became a prosaic and almost colourless activity.[6] Initially, the collective responsibility system worked well and kept individual ambitions in check, but after Deng died in 1997, power flowed out at a rapid rate. There were several reasons. China had always been led by strongmen who had had both revolutionary and administrative experience and commanded respect. Deng's successors, Jiang Zemin and Hu Jintao, however, had neither military experience nor a deep understanding of central politics. They were apparatchiks who had risen through the Party hierarchy in the relatively stable post-Mao period. They had spent considerable periods in the provinces. Jiang Zemin was transplanted overnight from the Shanghai municipality to the top offices of Party and state in 1989. Both Jiang and Hu were invested with the trappings of highest office – the general secretaryship, the presidency and the chairmanship of the Central Military Commission, which, theoretically, gave them commanding authority, but this was not the case in practice. Exercising control over the People's Liberation Army was an especially vital lever of power in China since Mao had famously declared that power grew out of the barrel of a gun.[7] Mao and Deng had kept strong ties to the PLA leadership, whereas under Jiang Zemin and Hu Jintao the long-standing Party–PLA combine was bifurcated.[8] The PLA grew more autonomous and independent, and by Hu Jintao's time, real authority over the army lay in the hands of generals. Likewise, the internal security apparatus also slipped out of their control. Luo Gan and then Zhou Yongkang, both of whom were responsible for internal security in the Politburo Standing Committee, became independent power centres. Cliques and factions, which Deng had always warned against, made their appearance. Jiang Zemin's own Shanghai faction was a major player in the dispensation from 2002 until 2012. The Communist Youth League (CYL) also emerged as an independent centre of power (both President Hu Jintao and Premier Li Keqiang were CYL members). The 'princelings' sought office in order to preserve the legacy of their revolutionary ancestors and to protect their rights to profit from the revolution.[9] Xi Jinping, Bo Xilai, Wang Qishan and Yu Zhengsheng were the most prominent members of this group. Jiang Zemin had also opened the Party's membership to private entrepreneurs in an effort to make it inclusive, but in time their wealth and influence also began to be felt in the corridors of power. Corruption and nepotism spread widely through the system, and it was reported that senior military positions could be bought.[10] Although Deng had not intended it to be so, power had become institutionally, fiscally and spatially decentralized.[11] Ideology or policy was no longer the basis for factional rivalry since there was leadership consensus on the package of economic reform and political stability from 1989 onwards. Instead, contests now appeared to revolve around the twin attractions of power and money.[12] The Chinese Communist Party seemed to become a motley group of power centres engaged in political compromise and coalition-building in order to maintain their hold on China.[13] For purposes of external projection, the Chinese leadership adopted the language and style of Western diplomacy. The shabby Mao suits were exchanged for sharp Western suits. The Hongqi automobile was replaced by the Mercedes-Benz as the transport of choice. Travels to the West were encouraged. Richard McGregor put it rather aptly when he wrote, 'In just a single generation the party elite has been transformed from a mirthless band of Mao-suited ideological thugs to a wealthy, be-suited and business-friendly ruling class.'[14]

The remarkable successes that China had in maintaining economic growth and political stability from 1990 onwards hid one major development. Communism as an ideology seems to have vanished in the Chinese state during this period. Mao Zedong Thought did not suit the times. The only ideology that was important was the preservation of the political status quo.[15] This trend seems to have gained momentum under the current Chinese leader, Xi Jinping. Outwardly, General Secretary Xi is viewed as having fundamentally altered Deng's carefully crafted political arrangements. His personal style of governance, the revision of Party rules and guidelines, the changes he has made to Deng's plans for orderly succession and the agglomeration of military, police and civilian authority in his person have attracted the world's attention. It is little appreciated that Xi has remained true to Deng's core message of protecting and perpetuating the rule of the Communist Party of China. Though his methods may be different, there is perhaps no real difference in substance between Deng Xiaoping and Xi Jinping on the core goal.

Since ideology has disappeared, notwithstanding the talk of socialism with Chinese characteristics,[16] the communist regime now seems to depend for its legitimacy on the economic numbers and nationalist sentiment. The Party claims that it is best placed to deliver economic prosperity and guarantee the security of the Chinese people. There is no doubt that the Chinese have prospered since 1990. However, it is equally true that the low-hanging fruit in the economy has already been picked, and China might face adverse currents in the years ahead. To meet the rising expectations of the people, China would still need to grow its economy by around 5.5 per cent every year from 2021 to 2049, which is no mean feat for a US $14 trillion economy that is already confronting a shrinking population, a declining workforce and falling household savings, as well as higher costs of social welfare for an ageing population. Sustaining economic growth into the middle of the twenty-first century will take significant reform and further liberalization. The leadership believes that the new policy of 'dual circulation' – a greater emphasis on the domestic economy over the export-led economy, the strategy of technological decoupling from the West and the creation of an alternative Chinese universe with the Belt and Road Initiative, an infrastructure development strategy which would connect Asia with Africa and Europe and promote regional trade – would enable the Party to meet the people's future economic aspirations.

Should its strategy fail, and if it is unable to maintain the economic numbers at an optimal level, China might have to fall back on the second pillar on which the Party apparently stakes its legitimacy, namely, Chinese nationalistic feelings. The Chinese people seem to have been raised on the belief that China was the worst victim of Western aggression and that the rest of the world owes it to make amends for the century of humiliation. The Party uses such nationalistic feelings as a tool for its legitimacy. Since the mid-1990s the Chinese Communist Party has used selective incidents to play the nationalism card, such as the bombing of the Chinese embassy in Belgrade by the US Air Force in May 1999 or Philippines' decision to seek arbitration on overlapping territorial claims in the South China Sea, in order to prove that they are the true guardians of the new China. The Party has thus increasingly linked its own survival to upholding the nation's honour and pride. The problem with this approach is that the Chinese government has had to escalate its response to perceived threats in order to meet public expectations that China's honour has been properly upheld. China has resorted of late to threats, sanctions and even military action. Chinese 'wolf warrior' diplomacy is the latest example of how the Party is being compelled to take ever more drastic steps to satisfy public opinion within the country, in order to keep their legitimacy. Should the economy stumble or fall, there is a possibility that the Party's instinct to play the nationalism card might lead China into a dangerous conflict. The risk of a minor conflict turning into a larger conflagration will be higher if only because the situation has got intertwined with the Party's own survival or preservation.

The remarkable progress that China has achieved should not hide the fact that it is not a fully normal state. It is a one-party state with an army that owes loyalty to the Party above the nation.[17] A proper understanding of the nature of the Chinese state is critical as China becomes a superpower. The 1989 Tiananmen Square incident, by offering a glimpse into the nature of Chinese politics under the Communist Party of China, adds to the knowledge about an institution that reveals little about itself even as it aspires to become the global hegemon by 2049.

Epilogue

THE FALL OF THE BERLIN WALL ON 9 NOVEMBER 1989, AND THE END OF Soviet supremacy in Eastern Europe the same year, turned the world's attention away from Asia and back to Europe. The happenings in Tiananmen faded from collective memory.

Deng returned to his original pursuit of modernizing China. His famous southern tour in 1992, known as '*nan xun*', ended any further serious opposition from the 'left', and put China on the path to becoming the world's second largest economy. He remained the tallest leader until his death five years later.

Even when he was alive, the Chinese Communist Party began a deep study on the fall of the Soviet Union. The collapse of the Soviet Union haunts them to this day. They concluded that Gorbachev's fatal mistake was to place glasnost before perestroika. It confirmed their belief that their actions were correct. The Party vowed that they would never allow the dictatorship of the Communist Party of China to be diluted.

Relations with the United States returned to the normal track. Within years the flow of trade and investment from America and Europe allowed China to achieve Deng's dream. The Chinese skilfully set out to convince the West that its rise was in their interest. It was the Americans and the Europeans who piloted the Chinese entry into the World Trade Organization, by buying into the Chinese argument that it was transitioning to a market economy. The Europeans tried hard to resume arms sales to China. The US thought they could mould Chinese thinking, to make them a responsible stakeholder. The Chinese played along, always following Deng Xiaoping's advice: 'Observe calmly; secure our position; cope with affairs calmly; hide our capacities and bide our time; be good at maintaining a low profile; and never claim leadership.' It has taken the West thirty years after the Tiananmen Square incident to realize the error of their ways.

The Chinese approached their relations with the West with open eyes. Outwardly, they courted and feted the West. Inwardly, they concluded that the United States represented an existential threat and resolved to tackle it. They are convinced that is the ultimate aim of the Americans – to subvert the Communist Party of China by introducing ideas about Western capitalism and democracy into China, until it erodes the ideological foundations of the regime. They know it as 'peaceful evolution', first articulated by Secretary of State John Foster Dulles in the 1950s. They completely distrust the Americans and are now in a position to challenge them in many areas.

China has undergone many changes on the surface. Its GDP has grown from less than US $500 billion in 1990 to US $14 trillion in 2019, and its people have become prosperous and proud. The Benz has replaced the Hong Qi automobile, milk products like ice cream and yoghurt are consumed with passion by a people who thirty years ago barely drank milk, and the Western suit is the preferred attire. But the Party still rules in China, and it is still helmed by the Red Aristocracy. It still places the Party before the nation. It still demands the absolute loyalty of the armed forces. As it celebrates the centenary of its founding in 2021, it remains determined to make China in its own image.

The students and youth have never again tried to protest. They may not have reason to. In the past thirty years, China has prospered and conditions have dramatically improved in universities. Jobs and prosperity have been delivered to the people. In return, they have surrendered some rights to the state. There are still those who dream of a democratic China, but most of them emigrate to the West and are irrelevant to most Chinese. There is no sign yet that the majority of the people want to exchange their present for a democratic future.

As for the foreign press, the self-appointed guardians of democracy and human rights in the world, to be a correspondent in China after 1990 was tantamount to a one-way ticket to success and glory. It was well known in media circles that it was preferable to cohabit with the Chinese foreign ministry if they wanted access to news. To be invited to tea with the Chinese spokesperson was not good for professional health. (Foreign journalists were only invited to the foreign ministry to be admonished or warned about their reporting. That is the case even today.) Most of them did not cover themselves with glory, giving a one-sided picture of China that was more or less in line with what the Chinese wanted to project of themselves to the outside world, though there were still some who wrote about the problems. I often asked them, when I returned to Beijing in the late 1990s, and again in 2016, about why their representatives in India were so critical on matters that evoked no similar reports from journalists belonging to the same Western media houses in China. I was loftily told that they held India to a different, higher standard. It is no longer possible for the Western media to hide their hypocrisy, and they have lost credibility.

∽

What happened to the dramatis personae in the drama that unfolded at Tiananmen Square in 1989?

DENG XIAOPING

Having successfully restored stability and order inside China, Deng was finally able to install a viable successor on his third attempt. Jiang Zemin was declared to be the 'core' of the third generation of Chinese leadership, and installed as general secretary of the Communist Party of China in June 1989, a position he held until 2001. Deng died in Beijing on 19 February 1997, just months before the return of Hong Kong to China, which counts as one of his greatest achievements. His family maintains that Deng never doubted his decision to use military force to end the stand-off in Tiananmen Square. His ashes are interred at the Babaoshan Revolutionary Cemetery, the Valhalla of the communist pantheon in China.

If Mao is acknowledged as the founder of the People's Republic of China, Deng takes his place alongside Mao as the maker of modern China. The reforms he initiated also allowed the United States and the West to enjoy two decades of unrivalled economic prosperity. History counts Deng Xiaoping as among the shapers of the twentieth century. His legacy is only just beginning to be fully appreciated, as the West wakes up to the fact that they acted as handmaidens to Deng in the creation of a China that is now on the verge of challenging Western hegemony.

ZHAO ZIYANG

Shorn of his titles and position, Zhao Ziyang still hoped for a rehabilitation of sorts, as had been the case with his predecessor Hu Yaobang. It never happened though, primarily due to Zhao's own intransigent refusal to admit his errors, as Hu Yaobang had done at a life meeting in January 1987, in exchange for keeping some of his positions and privileges. He and Deng never met ever again. He was confined to his home for the next fifteen years, during which he continued making attempts, in vain, to seek rehabilitation. He secretly recorded his version of events on tape before his death. It formed the basis for posthumous release of the book, *Prisoner of the State: The Secret Journal of Premier Zhao Ziyang*. He died on 17 January 2005 in Beijing. He was eighty-five. His remains were denied interment at the Babaoshan Revolutionary Cemetery.

HU QILI

Hu Qili's brilliant career and future as the heir-presumptive to Zhao Ziyang, as the general secretary of the Communist Party of China, died in Tiananmen Square. He was removed from all his positions in the politburo and its standing committee along with Zhao Ziyang, but unlike Zhao, Hu Qili cooperated by making a confession and was subsequently partially rehabilitated by being appointed minister for machine building and electronics industry from 1993 to 1998. As a post-retirement sinecure, he was appointed as the chairman of the Soong Ching Ling Foundation, and it is in this position that I had occasion to briefly see him when I was ambassador in China during 2016–17. Hu Qili still lives in Beijing.

LI PENG

Li Peng remained as premier of the State Council until 1998, but Deng's southern tour in 1992 would limit his power, and he would never again wield the influence that he exerted between 1988 and 1992. After demitting the office of premier in 1998, Li Peng was appointed as the chairman of the National People's Congress for a further five-year term until 2003. He died on 22 July 2019 in Beijing, unrepentant till the very end. He has been called by many names in the years after the Tiananmen Square incident, but the epithet that has stuck is 'Butcher of Beijing'.

THE EIGHT ELDERS

Chen Yun, Li Xiannian, Yang Shangkun, Peng Zhen and Wang Zhen, who together with Deng ended the careers of three general secretaries – Hua Guofeng, Hu Yaobang and Zhao Ziyang – all died in the 1990s, their power greatly diminished but their dream of the dictatorship of the Communist Party of China secure. Their descendants, known as 'princelings', are major beneficiaries of their political legacy and continue to enrich themselves.

Only two of the Elders survived beyond the year 2000 – Bo Yibo and Xi Zhongxun. The latter was believed to be the only first-generation leader who had had qualms about the handling of the Tiananmen Square incident. Ironically, their sons would be bitter rivals for leadership in 2011–2012. One, Xi Jinping, would ascend to the very top; the other, Bo Xilai, would plumb the very depths of prison hell.

THE STUDENT LEADERS

On 13 June, after the Public Security Bureau issued its most wanted list of twenty-one student leaders, only seven were able to escape arrest and flee to Hong Kong and onwards to the United States. These include Wu'er Kaixi and the husband–wife duo of Chai Ling and Feng Congde. Wang Dan was arrested and sentenced to four years in prison for counterrevolutionary crimes, and then arrested and sentenced again for demanding the release of political prisoners. He was finally freed and exiled in April 1998. All of them call the United States of America home.

FANG LIZHI

After Fang Lizhi and his spouse were smuggled into the residence of the US ambassador on the night of 5 June 1989, the Chinese enhanced their permanent surveillance outside the residence and prepared to negotiate with the Americans. Fang Lizhi was merely a pawn to be traded for other benefits. The Chinese drove a hard bargain. They did some tough talking with Scowcroft and Eagleburger during their first (of two) secret visit on 1 July 1989, without conceding anything on Fang Lizhi. Once it became public knowledge that Fang was inside the US ambassador's residence, the pressure began to mount on the Americans to ensure his honourable exit from China. The Chinese had the Americans in the perfect position to extract concessions. When Kissinger raised the matter with Deng on 9 November 1989, Deng said that he was ready to release Fang if he confessed. On 9 December 1989, when Scowcroft came visiting for the second time, hopeful of securing Fang's release in return for a confession, Deng wanted more – the lifting of sanctions and the resumption of World Bank loans. Since the American visitors did not have the authority to do so, there was no deal, and the US ambassador had to continue suffering the fugitives in their small residence. In June 1990, the Americans approached the Japanese and got them to promise that Japan would resume yen loans to China on condition that Fang be released. Deng got his deal. Fang Lizhi flew out of China to the United States on 25 June 1990, where he lived in exile and wrote extensively on the regime and its cruelties. Hardly anybody listened, aside from the left-liberal intelligentsia. A whole generation of Americans were too busy making money in China. Fang Lizhi died unsung in Arizona, United States, on 6 April 2012.

LIU XIAOBO

Liu Xiaobo was detained by the authorities for his role in the protests at Tiananmen Square. After his release, he was imprisoned again in 1995 for petitioning the state to reassess its verdict on the Tiananmen Square incident. In 2008, Liu Xiaobo was arrested for being one of the authors of *Charter 08*, a human rights manifesto for China. He was incarcerated virtually until his death in Shenyang, China, on 13 July 2017. In 2010, the Norwegian Nobel Committee awarded Liu Xiaobo the Nobel Peace Prize. It led to a nine-year diplomatic freeze in relations between Norway and China, during which the Norwegian ambassador Geir Otto Pedersen was unable to demit his position for fear that China would deny approval for a new Norwegian ambassador. It took the death of Liu Xiaobo to allow the relationship to be normalized in 2018.

WU'ER KAIXI

In 2004, I ran into Wu'er Kaixi on a street in Taipei. By the time I realized who it was, our paths had crossed. I could easily have traced his whereabouts, but did not do so, to my eternal regret. I wonder how much more interesting this book would be if I had spoken with him then.

Notes

Prologue

1. Mark Kramer, Steven Levine et al., 'Mao and the Cultural Revolution in China,' *Journal of Cold War Studies*, Vol. 10, No. 2, Spring 2008, MIT Press, pp. 1–2.

Chapter 1: The Principal Player

1. Benjamin Yang, *Deng: A Political Biography*, London and New York: An East Gate Book, Routledge, 2015.
2. David S. Goodman, *Deng Xiaoping and the Chinese Revolution: A Political Biography*, London: Routledge, 1994.
3. Ibid.
4. Ezra F. Vogel, *Deng Xiaoping and the Transformation of China*, Cambridge, Massachusetts: Harvard University Press, p. 42.
5. Scholars on Deng Xiaoping are divided over the reasons for Deng's absence from Lushan. Given the fact that he was a member of the politburo, it is unlikely that he could have unilaterally decided to stay away. It is possible that he used the pretext of injury to absent himself.
6. 'Speech Delivered at an Enlarged Working Conference of the Party Central Committee', 6 February 1962, in *The Selected Works of Deng Xiaoping: Modern Day Contributions to Marxism–Leninism*, Vol. 1 (1938–1965), Beijing: Foreign Languages Press.

7. *The Selected Works of Deng Xiaoping*, Vol. 1 (1938–1965).
8. Vogel, *Deng Xiaoping and the Transformation of China*, 53.
9. The resolution of the Central Committee of the Communist Party of China, titled 'On Dismissing Teng Hsiao-ping from All Posts Inside and Outside the Party', 7 April 1976.
10. Joint editorial in the *People's Daily*, *Liberation Army Daily* and *Hongqi* (or Red Flag), 16 May 1976, reprinted in *Beijing Review*, Vol. 19, No. 21, 21 May 1976. (*Hongqi* was the flagship magazine of the Communist Party of China until 1988 when it ceased publication.)
11. 'Decision of the Central Committee concerning the Great Proletarian Cultural Revolution', *Beijing Review*, Vol. 19, No. 33, 12 August 1966.
12. 'The Truth About the Tiananmen Incident', *Beijing Review*, Vol. 21, No. 48, 1 December 1978.
13. Jill Levine, 'Deng Xiaoping, Dazibao and Dissent: A Critical Analysis of the Xidan Democracy Wall Movement', *Senior Capstone Projects*, Asian Studies, Vassar College, April 2013. [Can be accessed at http://digitalwindow.vassar.edu/senior_capstone.]
14. Liu Xiaobo, *No Enemies, No Hatred*, Cambridge, Massachusetts: Harvard University Press, p. 42.
15. 'Leadership Politics in Post Mao China: The Fall of Hua Guofeng'. Research paper prepared by the Office of East Asian Analysis, CIA. (Declassified for release on 31 January 2007.)
16. Peter Harrold, 'China's Reform Experience to Date' (Washington, D.C.: World Bank, 1992), World Bank Discussion Paper No. 180.
17. 'Modern Shenzhen turns 40 and Becomes Focus for Xi's Tech Ambitions', Mercator Institute for China Studies, MERICS China Briefing, 22 October 2020.
18. Peter Harrold, 'China's Reform Experience to Date' (Washington, D.C.: World Bank, 1992), World Bank Discussion Paper No. 180.
19. *Beijing Review*, Vol. 23 No. 14, 7 April 1980.
20. *Vikrant* was an Indian defence magazine. It's editor Krishna Kumar interviewed Deng Xiaoping in 1980, which was published in the July issue of the magazine.

NOTES

Chapter 2: The Remaining Cast

1. Yen Lin Chung, 'The Ousting of General Secretary Hu Yaobang: The Roles Played by Peng Zhen and other Party Elders', *China Review*, Vol. 19, No. 1, Chinese University of Hong Kong Press, February 2019.
2. Li was trained as an electrical engineer and worked in the Ministry of Power for many years. In China bureaucrats are associated with a sector for years, like oil, power etc. and get recognized as such.
3. Alfred L. Chan, 'Policy and Elite Politics under Zhao Ziyang', *China Quarterly*, Cambridge University Press on behalf of the School for Oriental and African Studies, No. 203, September 2010, pp. 706–18.
4. David M. Bachman, *Chen Yun and the Chinese Political System*, Institute of East Asian Studies, University of California at Berkeley, Center for Chinese Studies, 1985.
5. Tom Cliff, 'Wang Zhen Rides Again?', in *Dog Days: Made in China Yearbook 2018*, ed. by Ivan Franceschini, Nicholas Loubere et al., Canberra: Australian National University Press, 2018, pp. 180–83.

Chapter 3: Storm Clouds on the Horizon

1. Albert Keidel, 'China's Economic Fluctuations: Their Implications for its Rural Economy', Carnegie Endowment for International Peace, 2007.
2. *The Selected Works of Deng Xiaoping: Modern Day Contributions to Marxism-Leninism*, Vol. 3 (1982–1992), Beijing: Foreign Languages Press.
3. Ibid.
4. Ibid.
5. *Beijing Review*, Vol. 28, No. 39, 30 September 1985.
6. *The Selected Works of Deng Xiaoping*, Vol. 3 (1982–1992).
7. Ibid.
8. Hu Qiaomu, 'Questions of the Ideological Front,' *Beijing Review*, Vol. 25, No. 4, 25 January 1982.
9. 'Key Questions in the Fall of China's Hu Yaobang'. Research paper prepared by the Office of East Asia Analysis, CIA. (Declassified for release on 22 June 2012.)

10. Yen Lin Chung, 'The Ousting of General Secretary Hu Yaobang: The Roles Played by Peng Zhen and Other Party Elders,' *China Review*, Vol. 19, No. 1, Chinese University of Hong Kong Press, February 2019.
11. Ibid.
12. Deng, 'Uphold the Four Cardinal Principles', 30 March 1979, in *The Selected Works of Deng Xiaoping: Modern Day Contributions to Marxism–Leninism*, Vol. 2 (1975–1982), Beijing: Foreign Languages Press.
13. *The Selected Works of Deng Xiaoping*, Vol. 3 (1982–1992).
14. Joseph Fewsmith, 'What Zhao Ziyang tells us about Elite Politics in the 1980s', *China Leadership Monitor*, No. 30, Fall, 2009. [The e-journal can be accessed at www.chinaleadershipmonitor.org.]
15. *The Selected Works of Deng Xiaoping*, Vol. 3 (1982–1992).
16. CIA report of 19 September 1986, titled 'Sixth Plenum to Showcase Hu Qili'. (Declassified on 12 April 2012.)
17. Zhao Ziyang, *Prisoner of the State: The Secret Journal of Premier Zhao Ziyang*, trans. and ed. by Bao Pu, Renee Chiang and Adi Ignatius, New York: Simon and Schuster, 2009.
18. Yen Lin Chung, 'The Ousting of General Secretary Hu Yaobang: The Roles Played by Peng Zhen and Other Party Elders', *China Review*, Vol. 19, No. 1, Chinese University of Hong Kong Press, February, 2019.
19. *The Selected Works of Deng Xiaoping*, Vol. 3 (1982–1992).
20. Ibid.

Chapter 4: Strong Winds

1. Gao Hua, *How the Red Sun Rose; The Origins and Development of the Yanan Rectification Campaign (1930–1945)*, Hong Kong: Chinese University of Hongkong Press, 2018.
2. After the overthrow of the Gang of Four in October 1976, China began to limp back to normalcy. During this period, a group of intellectuals and academics tested the limits of political freedom by voicing views on politics. Wei Jinfeng was the poster boy for this movement. After a few months this nascent experimentation was shut

down by Deng Xiaoping. This brief period in the autumn and winter of 1978 is referred to as the Beijing Spring.
3. Jonathan Mirsky, 'The Life and Death of Wang Ruowang', *Chief Brief*, Vol. 2, No. 2, 17 January 2002.
4. Fang Lizhi, 'The Chinese Amnesia', *China File*, 27 September 1990.
5. *Tiananmen Square 1989: The Declassified History*, edited by J.T. Richardson and H.L. Evans, National Security Archive, Electronic Briefing Book No. 16, 1 June 1999.
6. Chi Fulin, 'Symposium on Theory of Political Structural Reform', *Beijing Review*, Vol. 29, No. 46, 17 November 1986.
7. *Beijing Review*, Vol. 25, No. 50, 15 December 1986.
8. *The Selected Works of Deng Xiaoping*, Vol. 3 (1982–1992).
9. 'He Dongchang on Student Demos', *Beijing Review*, Vol. 30, No. 1, 5 January 1987, p. 5.
10. Zhao, *Prisoner of State*.
11. *The Selected Works of Deng Xiaoping*, Vol. 3 (1982–1992).
12. Life meeting is a periodic gathering of Communist Party cadres for criticism and self-criticism sessions. They are held to encourage introspection but are sometimes used to target cadres who are not in political favour.
13. Zhao, *Prisoner of State*.
14. *The Selected Works of Deng Xiaoping*, Vol. 3 (1982–1992).
15. 'Key Questions in the Fall of China's Hu Yaobang: An Intelligence Assessment', Office of East Asian Analysis, CIA, May 1987. (Declassified on 22 June 2012.)
16. *Beijing Review*, Vol. 30, No. 3, 19 January 1987.
17. Ibid., Vol. 30, No. 4, 26 January 1987.
18. Ibid., Vol. 30, Nos. 5 and 6, 5 February 1987.
19. *The Selected Works of Deng Xiaoping*, Vol. 3 (1982–1992).

Chapter 5: The Lull

1. Ruan Ming, *Deng Xiaoping: Chronicle of an Empire*, London and New York: Routledge, 2018.

2. 'Key Questions in the Fall of China's Hu Yaobang: An Intelligence Assessment', Office of East Asian Analysis, CIA, May 1987. (Declassified on 22 June 2012.)
3. 'Deng Under Pressure', CIA report, 10 June 1987. (Declassified on 20 March 2012.)
4. Zhao, *Prisoner of the State*.
5. Albert Keidel, 'China's Economic Fluctuations and Their Implications for Its Rural Economy', Carnegie Endowment for International Peace, 2007.
6. Zhang Jun, 'China's Price Liberalization and Market Reform: A Historical Perspective', in *China's Forty Years of Reform and Development*, ed. by Ross Garnaut, Fang Cai and Ligang Song, Canberra: Australia National University Press, 2018.
7. Albert Keidel, 'China's Economic Fluctuations and Their Implications for Its Rural Economy', Carnegie Endowment for International Peace, 2007.
8. Zhao, *Prisoner of the State*.
9. Kyochi Ishihara, 'Inflation and Economic Reform in China', *The Developing Economies*, Vol. XXVIII, No. 2, June 1990.
10. Zhao, *Prisoner of the State*.
11. *Beijing Review*, Vol. 31, No. 25 29 August–5 September 1988.
12. *The Selected Works of Deng Xiaoping*, Vol. 3 (1982–1992).
13. *Beijing Review*, Vol. 31, No. 40, 3–9 October 1988, p. 5.
14. Lowell Dittmer, 'The Tiananmen Massacre', *Problems of Communism*, Vol. 38, September/October 1989.
15. Ibid.
16. Fang Lizhi, 'The Real Deng', *China File*, 10 November 2011.
17. A common term used by non-Western diplomats in Beijing at the time to describe the motley group of people that Western embassies would patronize, as lip service to the promotion of human rights, in order to satisfy progressive opinion in their countries.
18. Interview with Winston Lord, Association for Diplomatic Studies and Training, Foreign Affairs Oral History Project. Interviewed by Charles Stuart Kennedy and Nancy Bernkopf Tucker, 28 April 1998.

19. Document 5, telegram from the US embassy to the State Department on 18 February 1989. US Tiananmen Papers, National Security Archives.
20. *The Selected Works of Deng Xiaoping*, Vol. 3 (1982–1992).
21. Ibid.

Chapter 6: The Spark

1. *The Tiananmen Papers*, compiled by Zhang Liang, ed. by Andrew Nathan and Perry Link, London: Little, Brown and Company, 2001.
2. Michael J. Berlin, *Turmoil at Tiananmen: A Study of US Press Coverage of the Beijing Spring of 1989*, Cambridge, Massachusetts: Joan Shorenstein Barone Center on Press, Politics and Public Policy, Kennedy School of Government, Harvard University, June 1992.
3. Ibid.
4. Li Qiao, 'Death or Rebirth? Tiananmen: The Soul of China', in *Beijing Spring 1989: Confrontation and Conflict*; ed. by M. Oksenberg et al., Routledge, 1990.
5. Ibid.
6. Kate Wright, 'The Political Undoing of the World Economic Herald,' in *The Pro-Democracy Protests in China: Reports from the Provinces*, ed. by Jonathan Unger, M.E. Sharpe, 1991.
7. Joseph Fewsmith, *China Since Tiananmen: The Politics of Transition*, Cambridge University Press, 2001.
8. Michael J. Berlin, 'The Performance of the Chinese Media during the Beijing Spring,' in *Chinese Democracy and the Crisis of 1989: Chinese and American Reflections*, ed. by Roger V. Des Forges, Luo Ning and Wu Yen-bo, Albany: State University of New York Press, 1993.
9. Dingxin Zhao, *The Power of Tiananmen: State-Society Relations and the 1989 Beijing Students Movement*, Chicago: University of Chicago Press, 2001.
10. Liang, *The Tiananmen Papers*, 135.
11. Berlin, 'The Performance of the Chinese Media during the Beijing Spring,' in *Chinese Democracy and the Crisis of 1989*.

12. Liang, *The Tiananmen Papers*.
13. Ibid.
14. Eddie Cheng, *Standoff at Tiananmen*, Colorado: Sensys Corp., 2009.
15. Zhao, *Prisoner of State*.
16. Liang, *The Tiananmen Papers*.

Chapter 7: Conflagration

1. Cheng, *Standoff at Tiananmen*.
2. Liang, *The Tiananmen Papers*.
3. Ibid.
4. Zhao, *Prisoner of State*.
5. Jing Huang, *Factionalism in Chinese Politics*.
6. The text of Zhao Ziyang's address to the Asian Development Bank governors was published in full by Xinhua News Agency, 4 May 1989.
7. Letter to Comrade Erich Honecker from Comrade Gunther Schabowski, politburo member of the SED (Socialist Unity Party of Germany) on his meeting with Jiang Zemin, 14 July 1989, Wilson Center Digital Archives.
8. Berlin, *Turmoil at Tiananmen*.
9. Berlin, 'The Performance of the Chinese Media during the Beijing Spring,' in *Chinese Democracy and the Crisis of 1989*.
10. Communique issued by the Third Plenary Session of the Thirteenth Central Committee of the Communist Party of China.
11. Liang, *The Tiananmen Papers*.
12. Ibid.
13. Zhao, *Prisoner of State*.

Chapter 8: The Blaze

1. *The Selected Works of Deng Xiaoping*, Vol. 3 (1982–1992).
2. Memorandum of conversation between President George H.W. Bush and Zhao Ziyang, 26 February 1989, Wilson Center Digital Archives.
3. Liang, *The Tiananmen Papers*.
4. Cheng, *Standoff at Tiananmen*.

NOTES

5. Liang, *The Tiananmen Papers*.
6. Diary of Teimuraz Stepanov-Mamaladze, 15 May 1989, History and Public Policy Program Digital Archive, Hoover Institution Archive, Teimuraz Stepanov-Mamladze Papers: Diary No. 9, translated by Sergey Radchenko, Wilson Center Digital Archives. [Can be accessed at https://digitalarchive.wilsoncenter.or/document/119287.]
7. Excerpts from a conversation between Mikhail Gorbachev and Rajiv Gandhi, 15 July 1989, History and Public Policy Program Digital Archive, Archive of the Gorbachev Foundation. Assembled from two (incomplete) copies, one available at National Security Archive; the other kindly provided to the author by Svetlana Savranskaya, and one (incomplete) copy published by the Gorbachev Foundation in Mikhail Gorbachev, Sobranie Sochinenii, Vol. 15, Moscow: Ves'Mir 2010, pp. 255–264, translated by Sergey Radchenko, Wilson Center Digital Archives. [Can be accessed at https://digitalarchive.wilsoncenter.org/document/119291.]
8. Meeting between Mikhail Gorbachev and Deng Xiaoping (excerpts), 16 May 1989, History and Public Policy Program Digital Archive, Mikhail Gorbachev, Zhizn'i Reformy. Vol. 2 (Moscow: Novosti 1995), pp. 435–440, Wilson Center Digital Archives. [Can be accessed at https://digitalarchive.wilsoncenter.org/document/116536.]
9. Excerpts from conversation between Mikhail Gorbachev and Zhao Ziyang, 16 May 1989, History and Public Policy Program Digital Archive, Mikhail Gorbachev, Zhizn'I, Wilson Center Digital Archives. [Can be accessed at https://digitalarchive.wilsoncenter.org/document/119290.]
10. Excerpts of conversation between Mikhail Gorbachev and Zhao Ziyang, 16 May 1989, Wilson Center Digital Archives.
11. Excerpts from a conversation between Mikhail Gorbachev and Rajiv Gandhi, 15 July 1989, Wilson Center Digital Archives.
12. Zhao, *Prisoner of State*.
13. Berlin, *Turmoil at Tiananmen*.
14. Zhao, *Prisoner of the State*.
15. Berlin, *Turmoil at Tiananmen*.

16. Liang, *The Tiananmen Papers*.
17. Zhao, *Prisoner of the State*.
18. Ibid., 30–31.
19. *Beijing Review*, Vol. 32, No. 22, 29 May–4 June 1989.

Chapter 9: Dousing the Flames

1. *Beijing Review*, 29 May–4 June 1989.
2. Berlin, 'The Performance of the Chinese Media during the Beijing Spring', in *Chinese Democracy and the Crisis of 1989*.
3. This is a personal recollection. There were many rumours going around Beijing during this time. There is a reference to this letter in 'The 1989 Tiananmen Square Incident: Retrospective and Prospective Considerations', written by Jacob Kovalio, published in *Asian Perspective*, Vol. 15, No. 1 (Spring–Summer 1991). Another reference can be found in 'The People's Army,' published in *Chinese Democracy and the Crisis of 1989: Chinese and American Reflections*, ed. by Roger V. Des Forges, Luo Ning and Wu Yen-bo, Albany: State University of New York Press, 1993.
4. Document 8, US embassy cable to the State Department, 21 May 1989. US Tiananmen Papers, National Security Archives.
5. Document 8, US embassy cable to the State Department, 2 June 1989. *Tiananmen Square 1989: The Declassified History*, ed. by J.T. Richelson and M.L. Evans, 1 June 1999, National Security Archives.
6. 'The Gate of Heavenly Peace', transcript of programme produced by Independent Television Service (ITVS) with funding from the Ford Foundation and the Rockefeller Foundation.
7. Ibid.
8. Berlin, *Turmoil at Tiananmen: A Study of US Press Coverage of the Beijing Spring of 1989*.
9. Liang, *The Tiananmen Papers*.
10. Document 11, US embassy cable to the State Department, 3 June 1989. *Tiananmen Square 1989: The Declassified History*, National Security Archives.

NOTES

11. See Amnesty International report titled 'The Massacre of June 1989 and Its Aftermath', 17 September 1990, which refers to use of weapons and ammunition by the People's Liberation Army. Also see *The Tiananmen Papers*, which, on page 383, subtitled 'Death on the Streets', says that bullets were fired on protestors and civilians.
12. 'The Gate of Heavenly Peace,' transcript of programme produced by ITVS.
13. US embassy cable to the State Department, 12 July 1989. Wikileaks Public Library of US Diplomacy.
14. See Amnesty International report titled 'The Massacre of June 1989 and its Aftermath', 17 September 1990, which refers to use of weapons and ammunition by the People's Liberation Army. In particular, Chapter 4 says, 'Numerous reports available from unofficial sources, foreign media and eyewitnesses indicate that during the night of 3 to 4 June some of the troops who entered Beijing forced their way into the city centre by firing both randomly and intentionally into protesters and onlookers, killing and injuring many unarmed civilians. Furthermore, random shooting by soldiers continued during the following days, causing more casualties among civilians.' Specific areas of Beijing where reports of firing took place have been named in this report.
15. Document 17, Secretary of State's morning summary, 5 June 1989. *Tiananmen Square 1989: The Declassified History*, National Security Archives.
16. Document 16, US embassy cable to the State Department, 4 June 1989. *Tiananmen Square 1989: The Declassified History*, National Security Archives.
17. Document 18, US embassy cable to the State Department, 6 June 1989. *Tiananmen Square 1989: The Declassified History*, National Security Archives.
18. Adam Lusher, 'At least 10,000 people died in Tiananmen Square massacre, secret British cable from the time alleged,' *The Independent*, 23 December 2017. The article quoted declassified telegram from

Sir Alan Donald, British ambassador to China, on 5 June 1989, UK National Archives, Kew, Richmond; London.

19. This is a personal recollection. Everybody who served in the Indian embassy at the time will recall it. Political Attaché Sikri's residence was hit by bullets. I saw the bullet markings personally. This incident is also referred to in the report, 'The Tiananmen Massacre Reappraised: Public Protest, Urban Warfare and the PLA', in *Chinese National Security: Decision-making Under Stress* (pp. 77–78), by Larry M. Wortzel, published by Strategic Studies Institute, US Army War College, September 2005. Another reference to this incident is in 'Document 22: Cable from US Embassy in Beijing to Department of State', Washington, No. 38, 7 June, 7 p.m., which may be accessed in the US National Security Archive website, George Washington University. National Security Archive Electronic Briefing Book No. 16 – *Tiananmen Square 1989: The Declassified History*.

20. Attributed to James Lilley, US ambassador in China. Lilley recorded an oral history with the Association for Diplomatic Studies and Training (Foreign Oral History Project), interview by Charles Stuart Kennedy, initial interview date: 21 May 1998, Copyright 2016 ADST, p. 145. His exact words were: 'The Defence Attaché Office had a guy named Larry Wortzel, who was a real "street man". He was down to earth and spoke Chinese well. Actually, he got a tip-off from a Chinese contact that the Chinese Army was going to begin firing at the Diplomatic Compound. We got some people out ahead of it.' Further down in the same interview, when Lilley is asked whether he knew they (Chinese) were going to do this, he replies: 'We had indications that this was going to happen. We saw armed people going into the building across the street from our diplomatic compound. We didn't know what that meant. Later we got a "tip off" that something might happen.'

21. Fang Lizhi, 'My Confession', *China File*, 9 November 2011.

NOTES

Chapter 10: Doubling Down

1. Liang, *The Tiananmen Papers*.
2. This approach was reflected in the Party's Four Cardinal Principles: uphold the principle of socialism, uphold the people's democratic dictatorship, uphold the leadership of the Communist Party of China and uphold Mao Zedong Thought (Maoism) and Marxism–Leninism.
3. Liang, *The Tiananmen Papers*.
4. Deng's idea of collective responsibility meant that each member of the Politburo Standing Committee (PSC) would have specific and direct responsibilities, but all leaders would own any decision taken by the concerned member of PSC. The purpose was to ensure that (a) power was not entirely centralized in one hand, and (b) the individual leaders understood that there was a collective responsibility for all decisions, and there would be no repetition of differences within the leadership as had happened in 1988–89.
5. 'China's Economic Rise: History, Trends, Challenges and Implications for the United States', Congressional Research Service Report, June 2019. [Can be accessed at https://crsreports.congress.gov.]
6. Lucien W. Pye, 'Jiang Zemin's Style of Rule: Go for Stability, Monopolize Power and Settle for Limited Effectiveness', *The China Journal*, No. 45, Jan 2001, University of Chicago Press for College of Asia and the Pacific, ANU, pp 45–51.
7. Address to the Sixth Plenary Session of the Sixth Central Committee, November 1938.
8. David Shambaugh, 'The Dynamics of Elite Politics during the Jiang Era,' *The China Journal*, No. 45, Jan 2001, University of Chicago Press for College of Asia and the Pacific, ANU, pp 45–51.
9. Mathieu Duchâtel & Francois Godement, 'China's Politics Under Hu Jintao,' *Journal of Current Chinese Affairs*, Vol. 38, No. 3, 2009, pp. 3–11.
10. James Mulvenon, 'Lawyers, Guns and Money: The Coming Show Trial of General Xu Caihou,' *China Leadership Monitor*, Fall 2014, Issue No. 45, 21 October 2014; Ting Shi, 'Corruption in China's military begins

NOTES

with buying a job', Bloomberg (online), 1 July 2014; 'Former Top China Military Official took huge bribes,' BBC News, 5 April 2016.

11. Shambaugh, 'The Dynamics of Elite Politics during the Jiang Era,' *The China Journal*.
12. Lowell Dittmer, 'Chinese Factional Politics under Jiang Zemin,' *Journal of East Asian Studies*, Vol. 3, No. 1, January–April 2003, Cambridge University Press, pp. 97–128.
13. Shambaugh, 'The Dynamics of Elite Politics during the Jiang Era,' *The China Journal*.
14. Richard McGregor, *The Party: The Secret World of China's Communist Rulers*, London: Allen Lane, 2010.
15. Ibid.
16. 'Xi Jinping Thought on Socialism with Chinese Characteristics for a New Era', or simply the Xi Jinping Thought, a new political doctrine derived from the writings of Xi Jinping in 2017, the supreme leader of China, which is currently taught in Chinese schools and universities.
17. Richard McGregor, *The Party: The Secret World of China's Communist Rulers*, in Chapter 4: Why we Fight; The Party and the Gun, 'The Red Army, later renamed the People's Liberation Army, was founded in 1927 as the military wing of a revolutionary party. Since taking power, the Party has worked overtime to ensure it stayed that way ... The founding principle of the People's Liberation Army, however, "the Party controls the gun", has never been up for negotiation. For all the recent focus on its growing global capabilities, the PLAs primary mission has always started at home – to keep the Party in power.'

Acknowledgements

I was not assigned directly to China after the completion of language studies in Hong Kong in 1984, as is usually the case, and instead was sent to Hanoi. But the outcome of my delayed posting to Beijing was that I was present at the events that transpired in 1989. I suppose I have my stars to thank for this fortuitous situation.

The book's origins lie in the intensive discussions that happened among the Indian diplomats posted to the embassy in China. We were very fortunate to have the guidance and wisdom of C.V. Ranganathan, the ambassador, Shivshankar Menon, the deputy chief of mission, and Jayadeva Ranade, the senior intelligence officer. Their insights and analysis have helped me immensely to build the backbone of this book. I am deeply indebted to all three of them for instilling in me the art of China watching.

My deep gratitude must go to Ranjana Sengupta, who, upon my retirement, encouraged me to write the book, guided me through the entire process and was always available to address my doubts,

ACKNOWLEDGEMENTS

of which I had many. Without her constant support and guidance this book might not have seen the light of day. In similar fashion, the encouragement and advice that I received from Navtej Sarna was a great help in steering me in the right direction.

I am thankful to the editorial team at HarperCollins for working on the manuscript in order to make it readable and comprehensible to the reader, a task that was made more difficult by the subject matter. In this regard my special thanks go to Suchismita Ukil, who painstakingly pointed out the parts of the manuscript that needed clarification and, in the process, also introduced me to the trials and tribulations of writing a book.

Finally, this book was possible only because my spouse, Vandana, supported me tirelessly through the COVID lockdown and its aftermath, and allowed me to devote time to my writing while she took upon herself the burden of doing my share of the chores. She has been my fellow traveller and we have witnessed the happenings in Beijing in 1989 together. It is, therefore, to her that I dedicate this book.

Selected Bibliography

Barth, Kelly (ed.). *The Tiananmen Square Massacre.* New York: Greenhaven Press, 2002.

Calhoun, Craig. *Neither Gods nor Emperors: Students and the Struggle for Democracy in China.* London: University of California Press, 1994.

Liang, Zhang. *The Tiananmen Papers.* Edited by Nathan, Andrew J. and Link, Perry. London: Little, Brown and Company, 2001.

Lim, Louisa. *The People's Republic of Amnesia: Tiananmen Revisited.* New York: Oxford University Press, 2014.

Tong, Shen. *Almost a Revolution: The Story of a Chinese Student's Journey from Boyhood to Leadership in Tiananmen Square.* Ann Arbor: University of Michigan Press, 1998.

Wang, Anna. *Inconvenient Memories: A Personal Account of the Tiananmen Square Incident and the China Before and After.* California: Purple Pegasus Publishing, 2019.

Ziyang, Zhao. *Prisoner of the State: The Secret Journal of Premier Zhao Ziyang.* Translated and edited by Bao Pu, Renee Cheng and Adi Ignatius. New York: Simon & Schuster, 2009.

Index

Aalto, Arvo, 39
agricultural prices, 45
agricultural sector reforms, 20
All China Journalists
  Association, 84
Altar of the Moon, xiii
Amnesty International report,
  160n11
'anti-bourgeois liberalization'
  campaign, 24, 81
anti-corruption campaign,
  25–26
anti-imperialist movement, 71
anti-party activity, 59
anti-rightist campaign, 23, 31,
  61

Asian Development Bank
  (ADB), 79, 82–83, 86, 100,
  104
Association for Diplomatic
  Studies and Training, 162n20
Avenue of Eternal Peace, xiii, 20,
  65, 73, 88, 105, 107–8, 120,
  122, 124

Babaoshan Revolutionary
  Cemetery, 146–47
Bao-Lord, Bette, 51
Beijing Military Region, 110
Beijing Municipal Government,
  104
Beijing Normal University, 65, 88

INDEX

Beijing Observatory, 39, 51
Beijing Review, 33–34, 98
Beijing Spring, 31, 82–83
Beijing Students Autonomous Federation (BSAF), 66–67, 71–72, 74, 89, 114
Beijing University, 52, 56–58, 63–64, 66, 71–72, 88–89, 92
Beijing University of Aeronautics and Astronautics, 64
Beijing University of Agriculture, 64
Belt and Road Initiative, 140
Benli, Qin, 50, 61–62, 83, 118
   reinstatement of, 74, 80
   removal of, 71
Berlin Wall, ix, 134, 143
Binyan, Liu, 27, 31–33, 36, 39, 83
'bloodletting', 127
Boli, Zhang, 114
Bonaparte, Napoleon, 63
bourgeois liberal intellectuals, 23
bourgeois liberalism, 39, 41–42
bourgeois liberalization, 12, 24, 26, 28, 36, 81
bureaucratism, elimination of, 27
Burghardt, Raymond, 128
Bush, George H.W., 52, 90

Butcher of Beijing, 148

Capital Iron and Steel Factory, 93
Carrel, Todd, 58
Castro, Fidel, 63
censorship on reporting, 71
Central Advisory Committee, 113
Central Bureau of Investigation, 86
Central Discipline Inspection Commission, 86
Central Leading Group on Finance and Economic Affairs, 46
Central Military Commission, 19, 116, 137
Central Nationalities Institute, 57, 99
Central Party School, 94, 116
Century of Humiliation, 1
Charter 08, 150
Chavan, S.B., 79
China Central Television, 120, 127
China Daily, 63
China Democratic League, 98
China Women's Daily, 83
China World Hotel, 105
China Youth Daily, 63
China Youth Political Institute, 99

INDEX

China-US relationship, 55, 90
   normalization of, 90
Chinese Academy of Social
   Sciences, 44, 92
Chinese Alliance for
   Democracy, 76
Chinese leadership, third
   generation, 118, 146
Chinoy, Mike, 74
CIA, 27–38, 112
civil war, 2, 14, 19, 110
Cold War, 21, 111, 130
commodity and energy prices, 45
Communications Research
   Institute, 99
communism, 79, 83, 139
Communist Party
   absolute rule of, 132
   adoption of capitalist system, 37
   apparatchiks, 76
   cadres for criticism and self-criticism sessions, 37
   Cultural Revolution, 5
   demise of, 24
   dictatorship of, 143, 148
   fate and future of, 44
   founders of, 79
   grip on power, 39
   inner workings of, 134
   intellectual needs of, 92
   key objective, 136
   liberal wing of, 61
   limits of tolerance, 15
   lost control over the cities, 99
   nationalism card, 141
   perpetuation of, 132, 134
   propaganda, 63
   reform of political structure, 35
   regained control over Tiananmen Square, 121
   secretive system of, 103
   step-by-step dismantling of, 88
   supremacy of, 9, 30, 67
   Third Plenary Session, 8
   Working Conference of, 4
Communist Revolution, 15
Communist supremacy, 26
Communist Youth League (CYL), 4–5, 14–15, 25, 138
Congde, Feng, 89, 114, 128, 149
consumer goods prices, 47
corruption, 15, 39, 81–82, 85–87, 99, 126, 86, 138
   public concerns over, 40
counterrevolutionary, 6–8, 68, 71, 74, 81, 118, 127–28, 149
   elements, 127

INDEX

political incident, 6, 8
turmoil, 68, 118, 128
credit tightening, 43
Cultural Revolution, 4–6, 8,
    14–15, 17–19, 22, 24, 32, 38,
    56, 113, 133
  ashes of, 15
  atrocities during, 75
  causes of, 23
  chaos of, 35
  cruelties of, 17
  excesses of, 32
  height of, 105
  labour camp during, 31
  mayhem of, 75
  standards of, 5
  survivors of, 19
  victimizations of, 5
cumulative impact of the
    reforms, 11

Dan, Dong, 67
Dan, Wang, 71–72, 74, 84, 89,
    101, 127–28, 149
Dazhao, Li, 79
Dehuai, Peng, 3, 96
Dejian, Hou, 111, 121
democracy movement, 74
democracy salon, 52
Democracy Wall, 7, 9, 30, 32,
    75, 81

political objective, 9
saga of, 32
shutting down of, 30, 75, 81
'democracy', suppression of, 5
democratic revolution, 83, 99
'democratic' upsurge, 132
dictatorship, 27, 31, 67, 99, 132,
    143, 148
Donald, Alan, 124
double-digit inflation, 20
'dual circulation' policy, 140
Dulles, John Foster, 59, 144
Duxiu, Chen, 79

economic policy, 17
economic reckoning period, 47
economic reform, 10, 22, 33–34,
    42, 46, 50, 82, 131–32, 139
economic restructuring, 48
economic troubles, 40, 47
Eight Elders, 148
Enlai, Zhou, 2–3, 5–6, 17, 19, 23,
    51, 57, 64, 77–78, 106, 113
export-oriented manufacturing
    units, 10

faulty banking and credit
    policies, 45
'Fifth Modernization', 8
Finnish Communist Party, 39
flexible wage structures, xiv

food shortages, 45
Forbidden City, xii–xiii, 1, 59, 108,
Foreign Affairs College, 94
foreign direct investment (FDI), 135
Foreign Exchange Certificate, xi
foreign invested enterprises (FIE), 135–136
foreign media movement restrictions, 121
foreign policy and external image, 12
Four Cardinal Principles, 9, 26, 132
Four Modernizations, xiv, 8, 17–18, 21, 38, 41
Fourth May, 79
Free Press, 124
Free World, 124
Freedman, Milton, 49
Friendship Store, 120–21
Fu Dan university, 33

Gan, Luo, 67, 138
Gandhi, Mahatma, 73
Gandhi, Rajiv, 13, 21, 94, 97, 125
Gang of Four, 5–6, 18, 26, 31, 56, 112
The Gate of Heavenly Peace, 84, 160n12

Goddess of Democracy, 117
Gongzhufen, 105
Gorbachev, Mikhail, 54, 66, 85, 90–91, 93–97, 100, 128, 143
  arrival in Beijing, 89
  historic visit of, 70
  welcome ceremony for, 93
Great Hall of the People, 50, 54, 58, 64–66, 79, 90, 93–94, 121
Great Leap Forward, 3, 18
Great Proletarian Cultural Revolution, xiv, 131
Group of Elders, 19
Guiding Principles for Inner-Party Political Life, 9
Guofeng, Hua, 6–7, 9–10, 148
Gupta, Shekhar, x

Haifeng, Guo, 65
Haotian, Chi, 119
'Hello Deng', 20
highest principle of politics, 132
Hong Qi automobile, 144
Huaqing, Liu, 119
human rights, 52, 129, 133, 145, 150
hunger strike, 89, 91, 93, 98–99, 101, 111, 114, 119
Hunger Strike Headquarters, 99, 114–15
Hunger Strike Manifesto, 89

[173]

INDEX

illegal student, 79
illegal unions of students, 127
Independent Television Service (ITVS), 160n6
India–China relations, 125
industrial overheating, 20, 43
inflation, 43, 45–47, 85
informal gatherings, 47
inner-party democracy, 4
inner-party struggle, 84
Inonu, Erdal, 87
intellectual property, theft of, 137
iron rice bowl, 46

Jianguo Gate, xi, 73
Jianying, Ye, 6, 12, 19, 23, 25
Jiaqi, Yan, 60–62, 91–92
Jinglian, Wu, 44
Jingsheng, Wei, 8, 9, 31, 51, 68, 75, 81
Jinping, Xi, 10, 138–40, 148
Jintao, Hu, 137–38
Jiusan Society, 98
Jiwei, Lou, 44
Juntao, Wang, 128

Kai-shek, Chiang, 2, 31
Kemu, Jin, 92
Keqiang, Li, 138
Khrushchev, 91, 96
Kissinger, 51, 149

Kumar, Krishna, 13. *See also* Vikrant
Kyodo News Service, 48

Law on Chinese-Foreign Equity Joint Ventures, xiv
Le Figaro, 99
leadership crisis, 112
Li, Wan, 12, 113, 116
Liberation Army Daily, 69
liberation struggle, 56
Lilley, James, 112, 125
Lin, Zhuo, 57
Lincoln, Abraham, 58
Ling, Chai, 84, 88–90, 93, 110–11, 114, 121, 127–28, 149
Liqun, Deng (Little Deng), 12, 23–25, 41–43
Liu–Deng Army, 3
Lizhi, Fang, 32, 34, 36, 39, 51–52, 54–55, 61, 68, 76, 80, 128–29, 149–50
Long March, 2, 25, 31
Lushan Conference, 3
Luxiang, Wang, 92

Mao directives, 30
Maoism, 11, 46, 132
Mao-style mass campaign, 42
Mao-suited ideological thugs, 139

INDEX

market-oriented policies, 44
market regulation, 22
martial law, 100, 103–8, 110, 112, 115–17, 119–20, 122, 126–27, 131
mass agitation, 11, 133
mass campaigns, 35
May Fourth Movement. *See* Fourth May
McGregor, Richard, 139
mercantilist approach, consequences of, 130
Ming Bao, 108
Mingfu, Yan, 91, 93
modernization process, 34
Monument of the People's Heroes, 57
Mu, Yuan, 76, 80
Museum of Chinese History, 122

Nakasone, Yasuhiro, 21
Nan Hai, Zhong, 59, 73, 90
'*nan xun*', 143
Nankai University, Tianjin, 64
National Opera House, xii
National Peoples Commission, 116
National People's Congress, 9, 60, 86, 107, 113, 148
nepotism, 40, 82, 138

public concerns over, 40
New China Gate, xiii
New Observer, 61
New York Times, 9, 83
1949 Revolution, 59
non-violent non-cooperation, 73. *See also* Gandhi, Mahatma

Office of Economic Reform Programme Design, 44
off-the-cuff policy, 15

Panjiar, Prashant, x
Party Central Committee, 22
Peng, Li, 16–17, 23, 43, 45–50, 58, 65, 67–68, 70, 75–78, 80–81, 85, 93–94, 98, 100–1, 103–4, 106–7, 109–11, 114–18, 148
People's Armed Police, xi
People's Daily, 31, 35, 37, 42–42, 68–69, 71–72, 74–75, 81–82, 84, 94, 109–10, 114–15, 126
People's Liberation Army (PLA), 3, 5, 19, 45, 63, 70, 78, 104–10, 114–15, 118–21, 123–27, 138
Peoples University (Renmin Daxue), 57
per capita incomes, xiv

Ping, Song, 44
planned conspiracy, 69, 71
planned economy, 18, 22, 44
Politburo Standing Committee, 9, 16, 43, 47, 65, 67, 78, 84, 86, 96, 98, 100, 103, 108, 117, 128, 133–34, 138
political reform, 24, 26–28, 33–35, 38, 77, 83, 86–87, 95, 132
political transition, 13
post-Cultural Revolution China, 63
price adjustment, 20
price reform, 22, 44, 46, 48–49. See also wage reforms
princelings, 17, 138, 148
Prisoner of State: The Secret Journal of Premier Zhao Ziyang, 147
pro-democracy slogans, 107
Propaganda Department, 24, 50
public messaging, 35, 78
Public Security Bureau, 62, 148
public transportation, chaos on, 113
purge of intellectuals, 32
Purple Bamboo, xiii

Qiaomu, Hu, 12, 23–25, 42–43

anti-corruption campaign, 25–26
Qichen, Qian, 109
Qijiayuan diplomatic compound, xiv
Qili, Hu, 23, 25–26, 74, 78, 84, 96, 100, 103, 108, 114, 147
Qing Ming Festival, 6
Qing, Dai, 91, 128
Qing, Jiang, 5
Qishan, Wang, 138
Qizhen, Zhu, 53

Reagan, Ronald, 21
Red Aristocracy, x, 26, 86, 145
Red Guards, 5, 31, 113
'rice bowl'. *See* Sichuan
right deviationist wind, 5
rightist intellectuals, 14
Rongzhen, Nie, 19, 23, 107, 118
'rubber-stamp' Parliament, 113
Rui, Li, 61
Ruolin, Wang, 77
Ruowang, Wang, 27, 31, 36, 39, 61
rural boom, 20

Sakai, Shinji, 48
Schabowski, Gunther, 82
Science & Technology Daily, 65, 83
self-perpetuation, x

INDEX

self-preservation, x
Shanghai, 6, 33, 50, 61–63, 69, 80, 107, 113, 117–18, 137–38
Shanghai Municipal Committee, 63
Shanghai Municipal Government, 62
Shanghai Municipal Party Committee, 33, 62
Shangkun, Yang, 12, 19, 53, 67, 77, 86, 91, 100, 115–16, 118, 148
Shaoqi, Liu, 3, 5, 7, 77–78
Shaozhi, Su, 50
Shi, Qiao, 23, 78, 100, 103, 117
Shuqing, Guo, 44
Sichuan, 3, 14, 16, 50
Sino-American relations, 15–16, 51, 54, 90, 130
Sino-Soviet normalization, 90
Sino-Soviet rapprochement, 66
Sino-Soviet relations, 95–96
  normalization of, 85, 96–97
Sino-Soviet split, 90
Sino-Soviet Summit, 78, 92
snow-balling effect, 92
socialism, 22, 26, 132, 140
  principle of, 132
socialist commodity economy, 44
socialist modernization, 8
socialist spiritual civilization, 12, 24
Socialist Youth League, 2
Soong Ching Ling Foundation, 147
Soviet Union, collapse of, 134, 143
special economic zones, 10, 133
spiritual pollution, 24, 30
Stanton, Bill, 128
State Council, 16, 44–49, 67, 75, 104, 113, 119, 148
State Education Commission, 17, 35–36, 55
Statue of Liberty, 117
student leaders, 148–49
student leadership, 67, 74, 89, 111, 115
student movement, 58, 71–72, 74, 79, 86, 89, 92–93, 100
student protests, 33, 36, 38, 43, 51, 58, 62–63, 65–66, 69, 72–73, 78, 80, 82–84, 95, 100, 113, 118–19, 126
Sung, Kim Il, 66
surplus farm labour for employment, 135

Taoran Pavilion, xiii
Thatcher, Margaret, 21

[177]

The Tiananmen Papers, 74, 76, 81, 83, 100
Tieying, Li, 67
Tong, Jiao, 33
Treaty of Versailles, 79
Triangle, 89
'Two Whatevers', 8

Uighur, 65
United Front Work Department, 91
urban price reforms, 43
urban reform, 20–22, 44
US Declaration of Independence, 58

Vikrant (defence magazine), 13
Vogel, Ezra, 2, 112
Voice of America, 123

wage-and-price reforms, 17
wage reforms, 46, 48
waihui. See Foreign Exchange Certificate
Wall Street Journal Asia, 80
Wallace, Mike, 28
Wangfujing and Xidan (shopping streets), xiii
Waterloo, Battle of, 63
Wen Wei Po, 42
Wenhui Bao, 6

Western journalism, credibility of, 70
Western print media, 106
Westernization and adoption of the capitalist system, 37
Western-style democracy, 26, 29, 58, 82
Wikileaks, 160n13
Winston Lord, 51–52
'wolf warrior' diplomacy, 141
Working Conference, 4
World Economic Herald, 50, 61–64, 74, 87, 107, 118
World Trade Organization, 136, 144
Wortzel, Larry, 125
Wu'er Kaixi, 60, 65, 72–74, 89, 93, 99, 101, 107, 114, 127–28, 149–50

Xiangqian, Xu, 19
Xianlin, Ji, 92
Xiannian, Li, 12, 19, 43, 51, 93, 113, 148
Xianqian, Xu, 107, 118
Xiaobo, Liu, 121, 128, 150
Xiaochuan, Zhou, 44
Xiaokang, Su, 91
Xiaoping, Deng, xiv, 2, 7, 13, 15, 24, 27, 31, 36, 43, 59, 94, 96–97, 100, 104, 106, 123,

INDEX

126, 128, 133, 135, 140, 144, 146
able leadership, 131
aphorism 'to be rich is glorious', 25
compatriots and detractors, 14
deliver dream of economic reform and opening China, 16
grand achievement, 97
humiliation, 97
leader-in-exile, 6
'neo-authoritarian' tendencies, 58
policy of economic reform, 4
policy of Four Modernizations, xiv, 8, 17–18, 21, 38, 41
post-1989 arrangements, 135
rehabilitation and reinstatement, 22
strategy, 135
Xilai, Bo, 138, 148
Ximing, Li, 93
Xingwen, Rui, 84
Xinhua News Agency, 59–60, 65, 96, 107–8
Xinhuamen, xiii, 59–61, 67
Xinjiang (Muslim-majority part of China), 19

Xitong, Chen, 76, 93
Xuezhi, Hong, 119

Yaobang, Hu, 3, 8–9, 13–16, 23–29, 32–39, 41, 43, 45, 49, 56, 58, 61–62, 64–67, 71, 82–83, 128, 147–48
as a political commissar in Sichuan, 3
breach of core principles, 49
confrontational tactics, 24
death of, 56
determination to allow freedom to intellectuals, 26
dismissal of, 35, 38
disregard Deng's advice, 27
general secretary of Communist Part, 9
induction into politburo, 8, 15
member of Youth League (1933), 14
memorial service for, 66
political ambitions, 23
political explorations, 27
political ideas of, 15
political judgement, 24
political struggle, 33
Yew, Lee Kwan, 21
Yibo, Bo, 12, 19, 37–38, 76, 148

Yijie, Tang, 92
Yilin, Yao, 44–47, 78, 98, 100, 103, 117
Yingchao, Deng, 19, 23
Yongjun, Zhou, 65–66, 72
Yongkang, Zhou, 138
Yun, Chen, 12, 17–19, 21–22, 25, 38, 44, 50, 93, 113, 132, 148

Zedong, Mao, 2–3, 18, 24, 57, 73, 77, 79, 96, 113, 132–33, 139
Zemin, Jiang, 33, 62–63, 69, 82, 87, 117–18, 134, 137–38, 146
Zengpei, Tian, 109
Zhen, Peng, 12, 19, 38, 93, 113, 148
Zhen, Wang, 12, 19, 23, 43, 93, 113, 148
Zhengsheng, Yu, 138
Zhili, Chen, 62
Zhongnanhai, xiii
Zhongxun, Xi, 10, 12, 148
zhuan lian, 113
Ziming, Chen, 128
Ziyang, Zhao, x, 3, 9, 13, 15–16, 27, 38, 41–46, 48–50, 61, 63–66, 75–82, 84–85, 87, 89–92, 95–96, 98–102, 103, 109–10, 115, 117, 128, 131, 147–48
  appeals to the students to resume their classes, 91
  appointed as party's general secretary, 38, 41, 45
  belated efforts, 99
  compelled to publicly reverse course, 49
  conciliatory speech, 84
  counterattack on political front, 50
  developed the national blueprint, 50
  direct appeal, 92
  economic policies, 44
  fall of, 131
  falling short on ideological and propaganda work, 50
  intransigent refusal to admit errors, 147
  joined Communist Youth League, 15
  meeting with Gorbachev, 95
  members of Politburo Standing Committee, 9
  official visit to North Korea, 65
  opening up a second front, 43

opportunity to seize, 85
political fortunes of, 89
political savviness, 80
position on economic
    reforms, 46

price reforms, 43–44, 47, 49
relieved of his
    responsibilities, 103
rivalry with Deng Liqun, 42
Zunxin, Bao, 60, 92

About the Author

Vijay Keshav Gokhale (b. 1959) spent nearly four decades in the Indian Foreign Service. He served as India's High Commissioner to Malaysia and Ambassador to Germany and to the People's Republic of China, and retired as the Foreign Secretary in January 2020. He worked on matters relating to China for a significant portion of his diplomatic career. His assignments in Hong Kong, Taipei and Beijing between 1982 and 2017, and his postings in New Delhi at various levels, have given him insights into Chinese politics.

Gokhale was present in China during the 1989 Tiananmen Square incident and witnessed many of the happenings. He regards the incident as a seminal event in modern Chinese politics, which ought to be studied for a deeper understanding of China. He currently lives in Pune with his wife Vandana, and devotes his time to the study of China.